Lift Up You

Lift Up Your Hearts!

A Collection of 30 *Khuṭbah* for Friday Prayer

Abdur Rashid Siddiqui

Foreword by
Prof. Khurshid Ahmad

THE ISLAMIC FOUNDATION

Published by
THE ISLAMIC FOUNDATION
Markfield Conference Centre, Ratby Lane,
Markfield, Leicester LE67 9SY, United Kingdom
Tel: (01530) 244944/5, Fax: (01530) 244946
E-mail: i.foundation@islamic-foundation.org.uk
Web site: www.islamic-foundation.org.uk

Quran House, P.O. Box 30611, Nairobi, Kenya

P.M.B. 3193, Kano, Nigeria

British Library Cataloguing-in-Publication Data
A catalogue record for this book is available from the British Library

Printed in Great Britain by Antony Rowe Ltd, Chippenham, Wiltshire

ISBN 0–86037–356–8

Typeset by: N.A. Qaddoura
Cover design by: Nasir Cadir

For the generations of Muslim students
of Leicester University
for listening to me patiently

and

For Asim and Shahla

Hoping that these *khuṭubāt* may inspire them

Transliteration Table

Consonants. Arabic

initial: unexpressed medial and final:

ء	’	د	d	ض	ḍ	ك	k
ب	b	ذ	dh	ط	ṭ	ل	l
ت	t	ر	r	ظ	ẓ	م	m
ث	th	ز	z	ع	‘	ن	n
ج	j	س	s	غ	gh	هـ	h
ح	ḥ	ش	sh	ف	f	و	w
خ	kh	ص	ṣ	ق	q	ي	y

Vowels, diphthongs, etc.

Short:	ـَ	a	ـِ	i	ـُ	u
long:	ـَا	ā	ـُو	ū	ـِي	ī
diphthongs:			ـِوْ	aw		
			ـَىْ	ay		

بسم الله الرحمن الرحيم

Contents

Foreword

Muslims are a faith-based community. Friday has a very special significance for them. The Prophet's migration to Madinah represents a turning point in the history of Islam. It heralds the founding of the Muslim community, the establishing of a society and a state on the foundations of Islamic principles and values and the induction of the Islamic *Ummah* as the upholders of the Divine Message and its witnesses unto Mankind (*Shuhadā' 'alā al-Nās*).

On the fifth day of the Prophet's advent in Madinah the institution of (Friday) Prayer was established by the Prophet, who led the first Jumu'ah Prayer at the habitat of Banī Sālim ibn 'Awf on the way from Qubā to Madinah. Ever since Jumu'ah has remained a key Islamic institution, providing the community an occasion for collective congregation, consultation and consolidation.

Prayers five times a day are offered in congregation (*Jamā'ah*) in every mosque in a locality but if one misses the congregation, the obligatory prayer can be offered individually. Not the Jumu'ah Prayer. It can be offered only in congregation and as such is a permanent institution in its own right. Jumu'ah provides an opportunity for all the people in a wider locality/habitation/city to gather together once every week to listen to the *Khuṭbah* and pray in congregation. It is offered only in the form laid down by the Prophet (peace be upon him). The *Adhān*, call for the Prayer, *Khuṭbah*, address by the *Imām* who leads the Prayer, and two *Rak'ah* Prayer in congregation with the *Imām's* recitation of *Fātiḥah* and some *Āyāt* from the Qur'ān in an audible voice constitute its main ingredients. The timings of the prayer is as that of *Ẓuhr* every day; but unlike the four obligatory *raka'ah* in *Ẓuhr*, Jumu'ah Prayer has only two obligatory *rak'ah* preceded by *Khuṭbah* given in two parts. These consist of *ḥamd wa thanā* (pronouncement of

Allah's Greatness), *ṣalawāt wa salām* (invoking peace and blessings on the Prophet), *Shahādah* (declaration of faith in Allah and His Prophet), remembrance of Allah, advice to the Muslims, sharing the message and meaning of Islam and its obligations, and supplications for the welfare of the Muslims. *Khuṭbah* and *Ṣalāh* are essential and inalienable parts of what has been called *Dhikrullāh* (Allah's remembrance) in the context of *Ṣalāt al-Jumuʿah* (al-Jumuʿah 62: 9–10). In fact *Khuṭbah* in two parts is the substitute for the two *rakʿah* waived in this prayer.

While every *Ṣalāh* is Allah's *Dhikr* (remembrance), the uniqueness of Jumuʿah has at least three aspects:

First, it represents a built-in arrangement for the education of the Muslims. *Ṣalāh* is preceded by *Khuṭbah*, whose purpose is to teach and educate the people in the meaning and message of Islam, to awaken their moral consciousness, increase their understanding of *dīn*, reflect upon the situation in which Muslims find themselves, share among themselves their concerns, aspirations and obligations towards each other and to humanity at large. There is an integral linkage between *Khuṭbah* and *Ṣalāh*, which sharpens the spiritual experience of the *Ṣalāh* and strengthens one's relationship with Allah and the *Ummah*.

Second, it provides the members of every community an opportunity to get together, meet and know each other better, share concerns and become more integrated and solidified. It is a powerful instrument for socialisation and cultivation of community life. The feeling of brotherhood and of oneness of the *Ummah* is strengthened. It also provides a forum for consultation (*Shūrā*) at the level of a locality and wider habitat.

Third, Jumuʿah represents the ethos of Islam *par excellence.* This is a day for special prayers and remembrance of Allah. The preparations for the prayer are part of the culture of the Jumuʿah. When the call for prayer is made, all business and worldly activities have to be stopped until the prayer is over. Listening to the *Khuṭbah* is obligatory, an inseparable part of the collective prayer and congregation. Any other activity is forbidden until the prayer is concluded. After the prayer, one is free to go back to one's business or continue other activities one is involved in. It is not a day to remain idle as in some other religions. Yet, whatever activity one is engaged in, Allah's remembrance is to be the guiding light. It disciplines the community to respond to the call, fulfil the obligation of collective *dhikr*, re-enter the business of life with full consciousness of what is good and as such to be pursued, and what is wrong and as such to be avoided. This is to be the model for the entire life of a Muslim and for an Islamic society. Life and its challenges have to be met, but met in a manner that conforms to the values and principles of Islam. That is what Allah's *dhikr* means and implies. Spiritual and material, moral and mundane go together. There is no conflict or contradiction between the two. If our mundane life is permeated with the spirit of Allah's remembrance, it becomes part of *ʿIbādah*. This leads to the spiritualisation of the entire realm of human existence. That is what Islam aims at, not dividing life into components of this-worldly and that-worldly, of religious and secular, but making them one integrated whole. Jumuʿah is the symbol of this distinct Islamic approach to life and the way its problems have to be faced.

The *Khuṭbah* of Jumuʿah is a unique Islamic institution. It represents a process through which the battery of *Īmān* is regularly charged and the current of Islamic life strengthened. The Prophet used the Friday *Khuṭbah* to convey his message to the people, to awaken their *Īmān*, to arouse them to good deeds and to inspire them to live a life in the service of Allah and His creation. His Friday discourses used to be brief, to the point and full of light and guidance. Unfortunately, in many parts of the Muslim world this role of the *Khuṭbah* of Jumuʿah has been marginalised or even lost. There is a need to revive the original spirit and role of the Friday congregation. The Islamic Foundation wanted to produce a set of model discourses that could become the basis for discourses on the occasion of Jumuʿah congregations. Our colleague and brother Abdur Rashid Siddiqui, has produced this small collection of such short *Khuṭubāt*. They are based on his Jumuʿah discourses at the Islamic Society of the University of Leicester. They cover a wide range of subjects, all directed towards one theme of imbibing the true message of Islam, lifting our hearts to become in communion with our Creator, becoming conscious of our role as Muslims and preparing ourselves to think, live and strive as good Muslims. Many Islamic concepts and fundamental values have been discussed with precision and depth. These also cover some of the special occasions and events that characterise Islamic life, e.g. Hijrah, *ʿĪdayn*, Ramaḍān, Battle of Badr. They are also geared to motivate one to learn more and strive to attain newer spiritual heights in order to fulfil our responsibilities. I have read these short and inspiring discourses with interest and profit. I hope they will be widely used by those who lead Friday Prayers, particularly in the universities, colleges and other gatherings of the youth. I also hope that Br. Abdur Rashid Siddiqui will continue his efforts to produce a second volume so that we have a set of fifty-two *Khuṭubāt* to cover the whole year. I pray that Allah gives the author the best of rewards for this useful service. May Allah give us all *Tawfīq* to live by the call of our Creator and Lord and follow the *Sunnah* of our Leader and Prophet (peace be upon him).

Leicester **Khurshid Ahmad**
20 Muhharam 1422
14 April 2001

Introduction

I thank Allah *subḥānū wa ta'ālā*[1] for giving me this opportunity to gather together this collection of *Khuṭubāt*. These are based on my Friday discourses given at the University of Leicester over the course of many years. Despite the promptings of many students to publish these some time ago, the decision to do so was postponed until my retirement from the University. This has now offered me the opportunity to look at them afresh and make the necessary editorial revisions.

As an Advisor to Muslim Students at the University for over two decades, I was responsible for conducting Friday Prayers. I have always encouraged students to give *Khuṭbah* so that people should not be bored listening to me week after week. The other reason being to encourage them in their learning of how to deliver *Khuṭbah*. Many were reluctant to undertake this, their excuses ranging from insufficient knowledge to lack of fluency in the English language. My hope, therefore, is that this collection will help equip them. I have also prepared guidelines for guest *Khaṭībs* who visit universities and deliver *Khuṭbah*. These guidelines are as follows:

- The purpose of *Khuṭbah* is *Tadhakkur* (reminder) and *Tadabbur* (reflection). "O you who believe! When the call is proclaimed to Prayer on Friday hasten earnestly to the Remembrance of Allah" (al-Jumu'ah 62: 9). This reminder should exhort the audience towards obedience of Allah and His Prophet (peace be upon him).
- It is essentially an *'Ibādah* (Act of Worship). Thus, people are required to listen attentively and talking during the *Khuṭbah* is not allowed.

1. This phrase is the praise of Allah and subsequently will be abbreviated as (*swt*).

- The *Imām* follows the precedent set by the Prophet (peace be upon him) and he should be very careful in what he says.
- For these reasons and also recognising the fact that our Congregation is composed of different nationalities, different schools of *Fiqh* and followers of different groups actively involved in the revival of Islam, it is essential that we do not raise issues that can be seen to advocate one or another specific point of view.
- Issues on which we disagree are very few and minor. Instead there is so much to say about those issues on which we do agree.
- Islam is a complete Code of Life. It covers spiritual, social, economic, political and legal issues. We can talk about any issue without provoking sectarian feelings. Some issues that we may feel are important but which are also controversial, require a different forum for discussion and debate where the audience can participate and air their views and ask questions of the speakers. Friday *Khuṭbah* is not the right forum to raise controversial issues where people may feel uncomfortable and forced to listen but unable to speak. The creation of such a situation is bad for the *Imām* as well as for the Congregation.
- Such controversial situations have sometimes resulted in fights in Mosques in both the UK and abroad. Sectarian killings are common in certain parts of the Muslim world. We should try to create harmony in the University. We should create a model of a peaceful Muslim society that despite the differences of opinion works harmoniously in presenting the Islamic way of life.
- As the time for *Khuṭbah* is very limited, between 15 and 20 minutes, it is essential that we do not exceed this time. Thus, it is not advisable to raise complex issues which need extensive discourse. It is also *Sunnah* of the Prophet (peace be upon him) that he kept *Khuṭbah* very short and relevant to the state of the community.

The above guidelines explain how I have tried to restrict my *khuṭubāt* to very basic Islamic teachings within the constraints of time.

It also seems appropriate to include some *aḥādīth* about the blessings of Friday and the importance of Friday Prayer and *Khuṭbah*. Our beloved Prophet said:

إِنَّ يَوْمَ الْجُمُعَةِ سَيِّدُ الأَيَّامِ وَأَعْظَمُهَا عِنْدَ اللَّهِ وَهُوَ
أَعْظَمُ عِنْدَ اللَّهِ مِنْ يَوْمِ الأَضْحَى وَيَوْمِ الْفِطْرِ فِيهِ خَمْسُ
خِلاَلٍ خَلَقَ اللَّهُ فِيهِ آدَمَ وَأَهْبَطَ اللَّهُ فِيهِ آدَمَ إِلَى الأَرْضِ
وَفِيهِ تَوَفَّى اللَّهُ آدَمَ وَفِيهِ سَاعَةٌ لاَ يَسْأَلُ اللَّهَ
فِيهَا الْعَبْدُ شَيْئًا إِلاَّ أَعْطَاهُ مَا لَمْ يَسْأَلْ
حَرَامًا وَفِيهِ تَقُومُ السَّاعَةُ

(إبن ماجة)

Friday is the most excellent and distinguished day among the days of the week in the sight of Allah; so much so that it excels both the day of *'Īd al-Fiṭr* and the day of *'Īd al-Aḍḥā* on account of the following five merits: Allah created Adam on Friday; He sent him to the Earth on this day as His vicegerent; Adam died on Friday; there is a blessed time on Friday during which a person is granted by Allah anything lawful and good he prays for; and Resurrection will take place on Friday.

(Ibn Mājah)

The practice of the Holy Prophet was that he would commence his readiness for Friday on the preceding night and would say:

لَيْلَةُ الجمُعَةِ لَيْلَةٌ أَغَر، وَيَوْمُ الجمُعَةِ يومٌ أَزهَرُ

(البيهقي)

"The night before Friday is a white night and Friday is a bright day."

(al-Bayhaqī)

It is also narrated from the Prophet (peace be upon him):

مَنْ كَانَ يُؤْمِنُ بِاللهِ وَالْيَوْمِ الآخِرِ فَعَلَيْهِ الجُمُعَةُ يَوْمَ الْجُمُعَةِ إِلاَّ
مَرِيضٌ أَوْ مُسَافِرٌ أَوْ امْرَأَةٌ أَوْ صَبِيٌّ أَوْ مَمْلُوكٌ فَمَنْ اسْتَغْنَى بِلَهْوٍ
أَوْ تِجَارَةٍ اسْتَغْنَى اللهُ عَنْهُ وَاللهُ غَنِيٌّ حَمِيدٌ

(الدارقطني)

The Friday Prayer is obligatory on every person who believes in Allah and the Last Day; the one who ignores it on account of sport or fun, or trade and business, will be ignored by Allah, and Allah is Self-Sufficient and Glorious.

(Dāraquṭnī)

The Prophet (peace be upon him) also gave a dire warning. He said:

لَيَنْتَهِيَنَّ أَقْوَامٌ عَنْ وَدْعِهِمْ الْجُمُعَاتِ أَوْ لَيَخْتِمَنَّ اللَّهُ عَلَى
قُلُوبِهِمْ ثُمَّ لَيَكُونُنَّ مِنْ الْغَافِلِينَ

(مسلم)

"People are warned against neglecting Friday Prayer, otherwise Allah will seal their hearts and they will be condemned to negligence (for ever)."

(Muslim)

The Prophet (peace be upon him) gave the following advice and guidance for the preparation and offering of Friday Prayer:

مَنْ اغْتَسَلَ يَوْمَ الْجُمُعَةِ وَلَبِسَ مِنْ أَحْسَنِ ثِيَابِهِ وَمَسَّ مِنْ طِيبٍ إِنْ
كَانَ عِنْدَهُ ثُمَّ أَتَى الْجُمُعَةَ فَلَمْ يَتَخَطَّ أَعْنَاقَ النَّاسِ ثُمَّ صَلَّى مَا كَتَبَ
اللَّهُ لَهُ ثُمَّ أَنْصَتَ إِذَا خَرَجَ إِمَامُهُ حَتَّى يَفْرُغَ مِنْ صَلاَتِهِ كَانَتْ
كَفَّارَةً لِمَا بَيْنَهَا وَبَيْنَ جُمُعَتِهِ الَّتِي قَبْلَهَا

(آبوداود)

> The person who has a bath on Friday, puts on the best available clothes, uses perfume if available, and comes for the Prayer, and takes his place quietly without disturbing the people, then offers the Prayer that Allah has destined for him, and sits in perfect silence and peace from the time the Imām takes his place till the completion of the Prayer, this will expiate all his sins committed between this Friday and the previous Friday.
>
> (Abū Dā'ūd)

Finally, on Friday, one should spend as much of one's time as possible in remembrance of Allah, recitation of the Holy Qur'ān (especially *Sūrah al-Kahf* and *Sūrah al-Dukhān* – as they are mentioned by the Prophet), asking Allah's forgiveness and doing other good deeds. It is useful to remind the congregation of this valuable guidance.

Those who want to use the model *Khuṭubāt* should start with the Arabic part of the First *Khuṭbah* given in the Appendix and recite the *āyah* as given at the start of the *Khuṭbah* and then read the text of the *Khuṭbah*. After finishing the first part the *Khaṭīb* should sit down for a while before starting the Second *Khuṭbah* which is also given in the Appendix.

In this first volume there are 30 *Khuṭubāt*, which are arranged in such a way as to convey the message of Islam in a systematic order. Of course this can be varied to meet local situations. It is preferable to deliver *Khuṭubāt* regarding Ramaḍān, *Ḥajj* and Hijrah at the appropriate time of these occasions. Jumu'ah Prayers are the only time when the maximum number of students attend the Congregational Prayers hence every effort is made to give them as much knowledge about Islam as possible in a very short space of time.

I am most grateful to Prof. Khurshid Ahmad, who has spared time from his busy schedule, for reading the manuscript and making constructive comments to improve and enlarge its contents. He has also kindly contributed a Foreword to this book. My grateful thanks are due to Dr. A.R. Kidwai for his helpful suggestions and advice. I have greatly benefited from the editorial suggestions of Mrs. Susanne Thackray. I would also like to thank Mr. Naiem Qaddoura for setting the Arabic quotations from the Holy Qur'ān and *aḥādīth.* Mrs. Debbie Robb rendered valuable assistance in technical editing and proofreading. Last, but not the least, I am most grateful to Dr. Manazir Ahsan and the Islamic Foundation for undertaking the publication of this book.

I pray to Allah (*swt*) to accept this humble effort. I hope students in institutions of higher education will find these *Khuṭubāt* useful and use them in their Friday Prayers.

Leicester
7 Ṣafar 1422
11 May 2001

Abdur Rashid Siddiqui

ʿIlm

ٱقۡرَأۡ بِٱسۡمِ رَبِّكَ ٱلَّذِي خَلَقَ ۝١ خَلَقَ ٱلۡإِنسَٰنَ مِنۡ عَلَقٍ ۝٢ ٱقۡرَأۡ وَرَبُّكَ
ٱلۡأَكۡرَمُ ۝٣ ٱلَّذِي عَلَّمَ بِٱلۡقَلَمِ ۝٤ عَلَّمَ ٱلۡإِنسَٰنَ مَا لَمۡ يَعۡلَمۡ ۝٥

Recite: In the name of your Lord • Who created, created man of a blood clot • Recite: And your Lord is the most Generous • Who taught by the Pen • taught man that he knew not.

(al-ʿAlaq 96: 1–5)

Praise and thanks be to Allah (*swt*), Who has created us and given us the faculties of reason and speech. He taught us the names and characteristics of all things in this Universe. He taught us the use of the pen and He taught us what we did not know and have no means of knowing.

May Allah's blessings be on our beloved Prophet (peace be upon him). That august personality who is a mercy for the whole world and the benefactor of the human race. It is through his teaching and by whose practical example an *Ummah* has come into existence of which there is no parallel in the history of mankind.

With the very first Revelation received by him in the cave of Ḥirā, was brought the message of *Iqra'* (recite). It reminded mankind of the blessings of both knowledge and the pen. Then it relates both of them to the Creator Himself. What better proof do we need of the value of knowledge in Islam than to know that the special task of Prophethood, which the Prophet (peace be upon him) was required to perform was the recitation of the verses of the Holy Qur'ān, imparting the knowledge and wisdom of the Book and the purification of souls.

Let us reflect on the verses recited at the start of this *Khuṭbah.* The very first word in the Revelation is *Iqra'* meaning read. This establishes the importance of knowledge. The first verse also mentions two attributes of Allah (*swt*). The first attribute is *Rabb* (Lord) and the other is *Khāliq* (Creator). It is instructive to note that in the Holy Qur'ān, Allah's attribute of *Rubūbiyyah* (meaning that He is the Sustainer, the Nourisher and the Provider as well as the Master and the Lord) precedes His attribute of *Takhlīq* (Creation). This we can see also in the beginning of *Sūrah al-Fātiḥah.* The reason for this arrangement is that a human being's first experience of Allah is through His innumerable bounties.

After mentioning these attributes of Allah, the verse continues to highlight the most important blessing, that is *'Ilm* (knowledge). Here, two methods of knowledge acquisition are narrated:

- Knowledge which one acquires through learning by use of the pen and paper.
- Knowledge which man did not know and has no means of knowing. This knowledge is revealed by Allah through His Messengers (peace and blessings be upon them all).

It should be noted that the Messengers of Allah did not attend any school or educational institution, yet they guided humanity by their wisdom and foresight. Their source of knowledge was Allah. This is further reinforced by the story of the Prophet Adam (peace be upon him). After the creation of the first human being Allah (*swt*) taught him the names of all things. This is mentioned in *Sūrah al-Baqarah*:

وَعَلَّمَ ءَادَمَ ٱلْأَسْمَآءَ كُلَّهَا ... ﴿٣١﴾

And He taught Adam the names of all things
(al-Baqarah 2: 31).

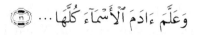

By teaching these names the implication is that He taught Adam the characteristics of all things as well. Thus He gave him superiority over all other creations including the angels.

Man was created as the *Khalīfah* (vicegerent) of Allah on Earth. Hence, it is essential that he should be given this knowledge so that he can perform his role of *Khilāfah* (vicegerency) properly.

In very many verses of the Holy Qur'ān, the superior status of those who possess knowledge is mentioned. Knowledge is referred to as *Nūr* (light) and *Baṣīrah* (insight) whereas ignorance is termed as *Ẓulumāt* (darkness). The word *'Ilm* and its derivatives occurs 778 times in the Qur'ān. This explains its importance in Islam. In several *aḥādīth* the importance of the acquisition of knowledge is emphasised.

The Prophet (peace be upon him) was sent down as a teacher. It is through his teaching and training that, within a hundred years, the map of the world changed with this new Enlightenment.

Thus knowledge is essential for being a Muslim. First we have to acquire knowledge – knowledge of Islam, and second we have to put this knowledge into practice. This is explained very well by Mawlānā Mawdūdī (may Allah have mercy on him) in his *Khuṭubāt* on why knowledge is so important for being a Muslim. A man can be English, Chinese, American, Arab or Pakistani and have no knowledge. Similarly, he may be white, black or brown and have no knowledge. His nationality and colour are something which he acquires at birth. But can a person be a Muslim by virtue of his birth? Is a person born into a Muslim family a Muslim just as a Japanese is Japanese because he is born in Japan or just as he is a Negro if he is born into a Negro family? I am sure you will agree that we are Muslims because we accept Islam as our *Dīn* – our way of life.

But what does acceptance of Islam mean? Surely it is not just recitation of *Kalimah*. The recitation of *Kalimah* is of course necessary for becoming a Muslim. But there is no magic in these words, which transform a non-Muslim into a Muslim. Surely no man can be a Muslim if he does not know the meaning of Islam. Because one becomes a Muslim not by being born into a Muslim family but only through consciously, with full knowledge, accepting Islam.

Thus, it is impossible to become a Muslim and remain a Muslim in a state of total ignorance. Being born into a Muslim home, bearing a

Muslim name, dressing like a Muslim and calling yourself Muslim is not enough to make you Muslim. True Muslims are those who know what Islam stands for and believe in it with their full consciousness. Sadly, many of us remain in a state of ignorance throughout our lives. We must realise that without knowledge we cannot truly receive the gift of Islam and its blessings.

You have come to this educational institution to acquire knowledge. You need this knowledge because it is beneficial to you. Without this knowledge you will not be able to earn your living in this world. Why then are you negligent in acquiring knowledge of Islam, which is vital for you both to live in this world and for your success in the Hereafter? I am not asking you to become scholars of Islam. Though some of you should become scholars of Islam as well. What I ask of you is to spend some time during your busy life in acquiring knowledge of this *Dīn*, which you profess is your Religion. Every one of you should at least have that much knowledge, to enable you to understand the essence of the teaching of the Holy Qur'ān and the purpose for which it was sent down. At least you should know what the mission of the Prophet (peace be upon him) was and how you should follow the path of Islam.

Let us pray that we realise the importance of Islam in our lives. It is essential for us to live the life of a believer. Let us resolve that we will find some time in our busy schedule to learn about Islam. May Allah (*swt*) guide us to the right path. (*Āmīn.*)

Islam

يَٰٓأَيُّهَا ٱلَّذِينَ ءَامَنُوٓا۟ ءَامِنُوا۟ بِٱللَّهِ وَرَسُولِهِۦ وَٱلْكِتَٰبِ ٱلَّذِى نَزَّلَ عَلَىٰ
رَسُولِهِۦ وَٱلْكِتَٰبِ ٱلَّذِىٓ أَنزَلَ مِن قَبْلُ ۚ وَمَن يَكْفُرْ بِٱللَّهِ وَمَلَٰٓئِكَتِهِۦ
وَكُتُبِهِۦ وَرُسُلِهِۦ وَٱلْيَوْمِ ٱلْءَاخِرِ فَقَدْ ضَلَّ ضَلَٰلًۢا بَعِيدًا ﴿١٣٦﴾

O you who believe! Believe in Allah and His Messenger, and the Scripture which He has sent to His Messenger and the Scripture He sent to those before (him). Any who denies Allah, His angels, His Books, His Messengers, and the Day of Judgement has gone far, far astray.

(al-Nisāʾ 4: 136)

In the last *khuṭbah* I emphasised the importance of the acquisition of knowledge about Islam. This knowledge is essential if we want to practise Islam. We say we are Muslims. Do we fully understand what Islam is? What does it mean to be a Muslim? We assume as we are born into a Muslim family and bear a Muslim name that we are Muslims. Of course most of us are fortunate enough to be born into Muslim families and brought up as believers. But as we grow up we have to make a conscious effort to learn exactly what Islam means and what our obligations as Muslims are. Unless we make a firm commitment to live the life of a believer our *Īmān* (faith) will be very superficial. For this purpose we have to build up our knowledge about Islam and try to fulfil our obligations.

The word Islam is derived from the Arabic root *Salamah*. The word *Salām* comes from the same root meaning Peace. In this way, a Muslim plays an important role in society. He is at peace with his Creator as well as his fellow human beings and all creation. The word Islam also means Submission. When we talk about Islam as a religion it means that we commit ourselves to submit to the Will of Allah (*swt*) and are ready to obey His commands. The opposite of Islam is *Kufr*. It means refusal to acknowledge Allah (*swt*) and His commands. Thus, if we were to ignore or reject the way laid down for us by Allah (*swt*) and decide to follow any other way of life we would be following the path of *Kufr*.

What can these other ways be? Of course as Muslims we do not deliberately try to deviate from the teachings of Islam. But people are influenced by the society in which they live. Human beings try to avoid conflict, thus they acquiesce to what is prevalent in society. There is a saying that when in Rome do as the Romans do. For young people there is peer group pressure as well. They do not want to be seen as freaks or out of step with the rest of their generation. Thus, they adopt the dress, outfit and speech as well as the mode of living of their friends. Some also feel shy about their names and try to change the beautiful names given to them by their parents. Thus, they have their nicknames which could be Sam, Riz, Mo or Bal instead of Samīʿ, Riḍwān, Muḥammad or Iqbal. They do not stop and reflect that what they are doing is not Islamically correct. Thus, the common malaise which afflicts Muslims are more subtle forms of *Kufr*.

Some people follow their whims and desires and thus they go astray from the Path of Islam. Allah (*swt*) says in the Holy Qur'ān:

وَمَنْ أَضَلُّ مِمَّنِ ٱتَّبَعَ هَوَىٰهُ بِغَيْرِ هُدًى مِّنَ ٱللَّهِ ۚ
إِنَّ ٱللَّهَ لَا يَهْدِى ٱلْقَوْمَ ٱلظَّٰلِمِينَ ﴿٥٠﴾

And who is more astray than he who follows his own likes and dislikes without any guidance from Allah. Surely Allah guides not the wrongdoers.

(al-Qaṣaṣ 28: 50)

When a person follows his own self (*Nafs*), his desires, and his likes and dislikes (*Hawā'*), then he is not obeying Allah (*swt*) but his own self. The reason for such behaviour may be to acquire worldly gain or to satisfy desires of his carnal self or to conform to society's culture. Such a person cannot benefit from Divine Guidance:

أَرَءَيْتَ مَنِ ٱتَّخَذَ إِلَـٰهَهُۥ هَوَىٰهُ أَفَأَنتَ تَكُونُ عَلَيْهِ وَكِيلًا ﴿٤٣﴾
أَمْ تَحْسَبُ أَنَّ أَكْثَرَهُمْ يَسْمَعُونَ أَوْ يَعْقِلُونَ ۚ إِنْ
هُمْ إِلَّا كَٱلْأَنْعَـٰمِ ۖ بَلْ هُمْ أَضَلُّ سَبِيلًا ﴿٤٤﴾

Have you seen him who makes his own desires his god? Will you be a guardian over him? • Or do you think that most of them listen or understand? Nay, they are but as the cattle; nay, but they are further astray from the way.

(al-Furqān 25: 43–4)

The problem is not confined to our younger generation. Some of those originating from Pakistan, India or Bangladesh were influenced by Hindu culture. We see very many customs reflecting that culture. Thus, many elaborate marriage and death ceremonies are not strictly Islamic. People blindly follow the customs and traditions prevalent in the society back home, although these may conflict with the guidance of Allah (*swt*). Still they are not willing to listen and change. When they are reminded that what they are doing is wrong, they repeat the old saying earlier Prophets were confronted with by the societies they sought to guide:

وَإِذَا قِيلَ لَهُمُ ٱتَّبِعُوا۟ مَآ أَنزَلَ ٱللَّهُ قَالُوا۟ بَلْ نَتَّبِعُ
مَا وَجَدْنَا عَلَيْهِ ءَابَآءَنَآ ۚ ... ﴿٢١﴾

When they were told to follow the (Revelation) that Allah has sent down, they say: "Nay, we shall follow the ways that we found our fathers (following)."

(Luqmān 31: 21)

The third cause of going astray is obeying other people instead of Allah (*swt*). People are overawed by the superior intellect of the West, even though such obedience conflicts with the guidance given by Allah (*swt*). As Allah said in the Holy Qur'ān:

وَإِن تُطِعْ أَكْثَرَ مَن فِي ٱلْأَرْضِ يُضِلُّوكَ عَن سَبِيلِ ٱللَّهِ ... ﴿١١٦﴾

If you obey most of those on earth, they will lead you astray from the Path of Allah.

(al-An'ām 6: 116)

If we take a critical look at the Muslim community we will no doubt come across all types of *Kufr* and *Shirk* (associating others in Godhead). When we say idol worship we think only of icons and stones. Yet these may be our own desires or the customs of our society or obedience to some higher authority. Unless we have firm belief in *Tawḥīd* (the Oneness of Allah) and firm commitment to follow His Guidance we can be led astray by the very many powerful forces we find around us.

The verse recited at the start of this *Khuṭbah* is addressed to believers. It asks them to believe! This may sound a bit strange but many of us who claim to be believers do not really fully fulfil our commitment. 'Allamah Yusuf Ali in his *Tafsīr* of this *āyah* writes:

> If your belief is by habit or birth or the example of those you love or respect or admire, make that belief more specific and personal to yourself. We must not only have faith, but realise that faith in our inmost being.

May Allah give us true *Īmān* and help us to follow the Right Path. (*Āmīn.*)

Īmān

ءَامَنَ ٱلرَّسُولُ بِمَآ أُنزِلَ إِلَيۡهِ مِن رَّبِّهِۦ وَٱلۡمُؤۡمِنُونَۚ كُلٌّ ءَامَنَ بِٱللَّهِ
وَمَلَٰٓئِكَتِهِۦ وَكُتُبِهِۦ وَرُسُلِهِۦ لَا نُفَرِّقُ بَيۡنَ أَحَدٍ مِّن رُّسُلِهِۦۚ
وَقَالُواْ سَمِعۡنَا وَأَطَعۡنَاۖ غُفۡرَانَكَ رَبَّنَا وَإِلَيۡكَ ٱلۡمَصِيرُ ٢٨٥

The Messenger believes in what has been revealed to him from his Lord, as do the people of Faith. Each one of them believes in Allah, His Book, and His Messengers. "We make no distinction (they say) between one and another of His Messengers." And they say, "We hear, and we obey: (We seek) Your Forgiveness our Lord, and to You is the end of all journeys."

(al-Baqarah 2: 285)

The words *Islam* and *Īmān* are sometimes used interchangeably to refer to our *Dīn* and Faith. But there is some difference between these two very important words. Whereas Islam is the Code of Life and System of Beliefs which distinguishes itself from other religions and ways of life, *Īmān* is the creed and Faith whose acceptance makes a person Muslim or *Mu'min.*

The Declaration of Faith: "I bear witness that there is no deity except Allah and I also bear witness that Muḥammad is His servant and Messenger" is the condensed form in which the complete creed of our Faith, as enunciated in the verse recited at the start of this *Khuṭbah,* is contained. On the basis of this verse and other verses of the Holy Qur'ān and *aḥādīth, Fuqahā'* – Jurists of Islam – have rendered this into six Articles of Faith. The formula is as follows:

> I believe in Allah, His Angels, His Books, His Messengers, the Last Day and the Predestined – whether it is good or evil – is from Allah, the Exalted and in Resurrection after death.

The *'Ulamā'* say that this creed should be sincerely believed in one's heart and recited by tongue and demonstrated by action. Only then is our *Īmān* as true Faith acceptable in the sight of Allah. Let us examine each of the Articles of Faith in some detail and try to comprehend what they imply.

1. Faith in the Oneness of Allah means that we believe that He is the sole Creator and Lord of everything that exists in this Universe. After the creation of the Universe He has not abandoned it but He is ever present and controls everything which happens in the vast Universe. It is He to whom everything living or inanimate worship and obey. Human beings are the only exceptions who have the volition to obey or not to obey Allah. By accepting Allah as Our Lord and Master we voluntarily submit to His commands.
2. Faith in Angels is also part of our *Īmān*. Angels belong to the Unseen World. They are created from light and, thus, are invisible to human beings. They are in total submission to Allah and are incapable of committing any sin. They have been assigned a specific task to perform in governance of the Universe. The number of angels is only known to Allah Himself: four of them, however, are well known, being nearest to Him. They are:

   First and foremost is Archangel Jibrīl. He performed the most important task of bringing the Message of Allah to His Messengers. He no longer performs this duty after the institution of Prophethood came to an end with the Holy Prophet Muḥammad (peace be upon him).

   Second is Angel Isrāfīl, who by Allah's command, will blow the Trumpet on the Day of Resurrection and bring the present system and order of the world to an end.

   The third is Angel Mikā'īl whose duty is to arrange for rainfall and the supply of provisions to the creations of Allah by His command.

And finally 'Azra'īl is the Angel of Death. He has been appointed to take peoples' souls when the appointed time of death comes.

Other angels mentioned in the Holy Qur'ān and *aḥādīth* are *Kirāman Kātibīn* – two kind and honourable scribes, and *Munkar* and *Nakīr*. The former are attached to every human being and as their names imply they record good and bad deeds. The latter are sent to the grave to question a person after his death.

3. Belief in the Revealed Books means that we accept that Allah sent down many Scriptures for the guidance of mankind and to teach human beings how to lead their life in the right way. The Messengers of Allah demonstrated, by their personal examples, the meanings of the Scriptures. Belief in all the Revealed Books is necessary as they basically identify the same creed. Five of the Scriptures revealed to five eminent Messengers are mentioned in the Holy Qur'ān. The Book revealed to the Prophet Ibrāhīm (peace be upon him) is called *Ṣaḥīfah*. The Prophet Mūsā (peace be upon him) was given the *Tawrāt* – this is the first five books of the Old Testament. *Zabūr* was revealed to the Prophet Dā'ūd (peace be upon him). This is known as The Psalms of David in the Old Testament. The Prophet *'Isā* (peace be upon him) was given *Injīl* – the Gospel which is part of the New Testament. And finally the Blessed Qur'ān was revealed to the Prophet Muḥammad (peace be upon him).

   Out of these Revealed Books only the Qur'ān is intact and exists in its original form and will remain so till the Last Day. Naturally, this latest Guidance from Allah has superseded all earlier Scriptures and their essential teachings are incorporated, without corruption into the Qur'ān.

4. Belief in the Messengers is necessary as they conveyed the Message and the commands for the guidance of humanity. We can only know Allah's commands through them. They provide the criteria for good and evil. If someone were to doubt their veracity and truthfulness then the truth of the Divine Message would be in doubt as well. Allah has sent Messengers throughout the ages to all parts of the world to guide human beings. Obedience to the Prophet is indeed obedience to Allah and disobedience of the Prophet is disobedience of Allah. Love of Allah demands that one should obey

the Prophet for that alone is the test of one's firmness in Faith. The exact number of Prophets is not known. In some *aḥādīth* a figure of 124,000 is mentioned. In the Holy Qur'ān, only 25 are mentioned by name.

5. Belief in the Last Day makes us realise that this world is transitory and will end one day. On that day, all creation will be destroyed and people will be raised from their graves. They will stand before their Lord who will judge their deeds. Thereafter people will be rewarded or punished according to their deeds. This accountability before Allah keeps people on the Path of Righteousness and steadfast in their *Īmān*.
6. Belief in *Taqdīr* – destiny – means that whatever happens emanates from Almighty Allah. This belief makes one totally dependent on the Will of Allah (*swt*). It provides inner strength to forbear all miseries and calamities in life. One should be neither despondent nor despair but instead always hopeful that Allah will change the situation. Allah controls all affairs and nothing happens in this Universe which is not by His prior knowledge. The duty of human beings is to make their utmost effort and then be hopeful of Allah's help.

These six Articles of Faith are subsumed in essentially the three fundamental beliefs of *Tawḥīd, Risālah* and *Ākhirah* that is belief in the Oneness of Allah, Prophethood and the Hereafter. The entire edifice of Islamic civilisation is based on these fundamental beliefs. If *Īmān* were weak it not only weakens beliefs, but it destroys morality, social structure and the entire culture and civilisation of Muslims. It is for this reason that the difference between Islam and *Kufr* rests on *Īmān*.

Let us earnestly pray that Allah, the Most Kind and Most Merciful strengthens our *Īmān* and gives us firm Faith and conviction in our beliefs. (*Āmīn.*)

Tawḥīd

ٱللَّهُ لَآ إِلَٰهَ إِلَّا هُوَ ٱلْحَىُّ ٱلْقَيُّومُ ۚ لَا تَأْخُذُهُۥ سِنَةٌ وَلَا نَوْمٌ ۚ لَّهُۥ
مَا فِى ٱلسَّمَٰوَٰتِ وَمَا فِى ٱلْأَرْضِ ۗ مَن ذَا ٱلَّذِى يَشْفَعُ عِندَهُۥٓ إِلَّا
بِإِذْنِهِۦ ۚ يَعْلَمُ مَا بَيْنَ أَيْدِيهِمْ وَمَا خَلْفَهُمْ ۖ وَلَا يُحِيطُونَ
بِشَىْءٍ مِّنْ عِلْمِهِۦٓ إِلَّا بِمَا شَآءَ ۚ وَسِعَ كُرْسِيُّهُ ٱلسَّمَٰوَٰتِ
وَٱلْأَرْضَ ۖ وَلَا يَـُٔودُهُۥ حِفْظُهُمَا ۚ وَهُوَ ٱلْعَلِىُّ ٱلْعَظِيمُ ﴿٢٥٥﴾

Allah! There is no god save Him, the Alive, the Eternal. Neither slumber nor sleep overtakes Him. Unto Him belongs whatsoever is in the heavens and whatsoever is in the earth. Who is he that intercedes with Him except by His permission? He knows that which is in front of them and that which is behind them, while they encompass nothing of His knowledge except what He will. His Throne includes the heavens and the earth, and He is never weary of preserving them. He is Sublime, the Almighty.

(al-Baqarah 2: 255)

The Islamic creed is based on a clear statement – *Lā ilāha illal-Lāh* – There is no deity except Allah. This declaration of Faith leads a Muslim throughout his life. Belief in Allah is the basic concept of Islam. Belief in the Oneness of Allah, which is termed *Tawḥīd* in Arabic, is the foundation stone of the Faith.

The word Allah is unique and almost incapable of being translated into any other language. The English word God with a capital "G" does not convey the actual meaning of the word Allah. It is the proper noun for the Ultimate Reality in this Universe. Thus, we cannot have the plural of this word just as "god" with a small "g" becomes gods nor can we turn it into the feminine form as goddess. Allah also means "one who deserved to be loved" and "unto whom everyone seeks refuge". He is One and the Only One who deserves all praises and all thanks.

The concept of the Oneness of Allah is called *Tawḥīd.* This conveys the idea of God as a Single Entity. The Qur'ān does not give any details about the Being or Essence of God, as this is beyond human comprehension and understanding. There are many verses that convey this to us:

لَيْسَ كَمِثْلِهِۦ شَىْءٌ ۖ وَهُوَ ٱلسَّمِيعُ ٱلْبَصِيرُ ﴿١١﴾

There is nothing whatever like Him.

(al-Shūrā 42: 11)

لَّا تُدْرِكُهُ ٱلْأَبْصَٰرُ ... ﴿١٠٣﴾

Eyes cannot perceive Him.

(al-An'ām 6: 103)

Thus, we are asked not to reflect on the person of Allah but to contemplate on His beautiful and perfect Attributes called *Asmā' al-ḥusnā*. It is narrated by Abū Hurairah (may Allah be pleased with him) that the Prophet (peace be upon him) said:

إِنَّ لِلّهِ تِسْعَةً وَتِسْعِينَ اسْمًا مَنْ أَحْصَاهَا دَخَلَ الْجَنَّةَ

(متفق عليه)

Verily, there are ninety-nine Names of God, whosoever recites them shall enter Paradise.

(Bukhārī and Muslim)

These Names express the Attributes of Allah. They lead us to a correct understanding of our relationship with Allah. They allow us to focus on His Attributes and fashion our lives accordingly. The very first words which we read when we open the Book of Allah, the Blessed Qur'ān, are:

بِسْمِ اللهِ الرَّحْمَـٰنِ الرَّحِيـمِ

In the name of Allah, the Merciful, the Beneficent.

Al-Raḥmān and *Al-Raḥīm* express the immensity of Divine Mercy for everything that is in the Universe. *Al-Raḥmān* is also another proper noun for Allah as it connotes the overwhelming outflow of Mercy. This term is too strong and powerful to be used for human beings. Allah's Mercy (*Raḥmah*) engulfs everything. Thus, when we recite *al-Raḥmān* and *al-Raḥīm* we realise that God's relationship with His creature is of love, sympathy, concern, compassion and mercy. Thus, the concept of God in Islam is above all other Attributes, that of His being, Merciful, Compassionate and Beneficent.

Some of His other Attributes are:

al-Ḥakīm	The Wise
al-'Ālim	The All-Knower
al-Ghafūr	The Forgiving
al-Khāliq	The Creator
al-'Azīz	The All-Powerful
al-Samī'	The All-Hearing
al-Baṣīr	The All-Seeing

In light of these and other Attributes we can forge a very strong relationship with Allah and, thus, develop and mould ourselves.

A human being, having limited knowledge, is incapable of formulating everlasting principles to govern his life on this Earth. He cannot create balance and harmony within society so that they can be in equilibrium with the rest of the Universe. Because of our limited foresight and vision we need Allah's Guidance and Help to live in this world. Thus, Allah, in all His Mercy, has sent down Prophets throughout the ages who guided mankind to the Right Path. But many times in the past people turned away from *Tawḥīd* and began to associate others in Godhead. This is called *Shirk.* This can be worshipping any person or creature or even inanimate objects or seeking help from others instead of Allah. In the past, there were Greek and Roman gods and goddesses like Apollo, Hades, Diana or Aphrodite and others. Hindus even today worship Shiva, Kali and Lakshami and thousands of other deities.

In our modern era instead of idols of stone there are different ideologies like Nationalism, Capitalism and Socialism to which people pay their allegiance. Islamic teaching conversely is that the One who has created is the Real Sovereign. He governs the whole Universe and His laws should be observed in all our affairs. Allah says in the Qur'ān:

أَلَا لَهُ ٱلْخَلْقُ وَٱلْأَمْرُ ۗ تَبَارَكَ ٱللَّهُ رَبُّ ٱلْعَٰلَمِينَ ﴿٥٤﴾

Lo! His is the creation and His is the command. Blessed is Allah, the Lord of the universe.

(al-A'rāf 7: 54)

إِنِ ٱلْحُكْمُ إِلَّا لِلَّهِ ۚ أَمَرَ أَلَّا تَعْبُدُوٓا۟ إِلَّآ إِيَّاهُ ۚ ذَٰلِكَ ٱلدِّينُ ٱلْقَيِّمُ
وَلَٰكِنَّ أَكْثَرَ ٱلنَّاسِ لَا يَعْلَمُونَ ﴿٤٠﴾

The Command is for none but Allah. He has commanded that you worship none but Him. That is the right Dīn, *but many people do not understand this.*

(Yūsuf 12: 40)

Thus, it is the prerogative of Allah to declare what is lawful and what is unlawful. He alone can lay down laws for our guidance. He alone has a right to legislate for us. Just as He alone is to be worshipped.

These are some of the most important implications of saying *Lā ilāha illal-Lāh* – There is no deity except Allah.

As Prof. Khurshid Ahmad writes in *Islam: Its Meaning and Message*:

> But it (*Tawḥīd*) is not merely a metaphysical concept. It is dynamic belief and a revolutionary doctrine. It means that all men are the creatures of one God – they are equal. Discrimination based on colour, class, race or territory is unfounded and illusory.

> It is a remnant of the days of ignorance, which chained men down to servitude. Humanity is one single family of God and there can be no sanction for those barriers. Men are one – and not bourgeois or proletarian, white or black, Aryan or non-Aryan, Westerner or Easterner. Islam gives a revolutionary concept of the unity of mankind (p.30).

May Allah guide us and help us to fulfil the obligations of our *Īmān*. (*Āmīn.*)

Risālah

وَلِكُلِّ أُمَّةٍ رَّسُولٌ ۖ فَإِذَا جَآءَ رَسُولُهُمْ قُضِىَ بَيْنَهُم
بِٱلْقِسْطِ وَهُمْ لَا يُظْلَمُونَ ﴿٤٧﴾

To every nation (was sent) a Messenger: when their Messenger comes (before them), the matter will be judged between them with justice, and they will not be wronged.
(Yūnus 10: 47)

Belief in Prophets and Messengers is an important doctrine in Islam. Prophethood is a bounty and a favour from Allah. He bestows this honour to whomsoever He pleases. As it is a Divine appointment, it cannot be acquired by anyone's personal effort, however pious he may be. Although Prophets are held in the highest esteem they are chosen from human beings and, thus, are liable to feel pain and hurt like anyone else. The only difference which elevates them above others is that they receive Guidance from Allah as mentioned in the Holy Qur'ān:

قُلْ إِنَّمَآ أَنَا۠ بَشَرٌ مِّثْلُكُمْ يُوحَىٰٓ إِلَىَّ ... ﴿١١٠﴾

Say: "I am a man like yourselves, (but) the Revelation has come to me."
(al-Kahf 18: 110)

The words Prophets and Messengers are commonly used interchangeably. However there is a slight difference between a Messenger (*Rasūl*) and a Prophet (*Nabī*). A Messenger is a Prophet who is given

Divine Guidance in the form of Scriptures, whereas Prophets who come in the periods between Messengers follow the Divine Book of the preceding Messenger. Thus, all Messengers are *Rasūl* and *Nabī* but all Prophets are not *Rasūl* (Messenger). As all Messengers and Prophets are honoured by Allah, it is customary to say and write *'Alaihis Salām* (peace be on him) after their names.

All Messengers and Prophets brought the same *Dīn* (Religion, way of life) for mankind. Their basic teachings were the same. They called upon mankind, saying:

إِنِّي لَكُمْ رَسُولٌ أَمِينٌ ﴿١٦٢﴾ فَاتَّقُوا اللَّهَ وَأَطِيعُونِ ﴿١٦٣﴾

I am a Messenger worthy of all trust. So fear Allah and obey me.

(al-Shu'arā' 26: 162–3)

Of course the *Sharī'ah* (laws and regulations) differ from one Messenger to the next due to changes in situations.

People sometimes question the need for Messengers. They say: "We do not need a Messenger for our guidance as we are mature enough to find out our own way." This attitude is one of sheer arrogance, as we know very well, despite our scientific and technological progress, we still have glaring gaps in our knowledge. We are motivated by our selfish interests of nationalism, racism, linguistic and colour prejudices. Thus, we waiver in our opinions from one extreme to the other and fail to grasp the Straight Path, *Ṣirāṭ al-Mustaqīm*.

Some people object to the fact that Messengers and Prophets were all human beings. They think such persons should have been angels or at least human beings with superhuman qualities. Thus, they should be different from ordinary human beings. But a little reflection will show the fallacy of such an argument. As Messengers and Prophets were models for humanity, how could people follow their examples if they were angels or super beings? Then, people would have argued, it is all very well for angels and super beings to follow the Path of Righteousness but we cannot be expected to achieve their standards.

Allah has provided for all our physical needs. We cultivate crops and tame animals for our food. We build shelters and houses. We spin cotton and wool to clothe ourselves and make tools to make life comfortable. For doing these worldly chores, Allah has given us enough knowledge to survive on earth. What we need is moral and spiritual guidance. Thus, the first person who was created was also designated a Prophet (Adam *'alaihis salām*). He was promised that:

يَـٰبَنِىٓ ءَادَمَ إِمَّا يَأْتِيَنَّكُمْ رُسُلٌ مِّنكُمْ يَقُصُّونَ عَلَيْكُمْ ءَايَـٰتِى فَمَنِ
ٱتَّقَىٰ وَأَصْلَحَ فَلَا خَوْفٌ عَلَيْهِمْ وَلَا هُمْ يَحْزَنُونَ ﴿٣٥﴾

O you Children of Adam! Whenever there come to you Messengers from amongst you, rehearsing My Signs unto you – those who are righteous and mend (their lives) – on them shall be no fear nor shall they grieve.

(al-A'rāf 7: 35)

Thus, it is obligatory to believe in the Messengers of Allah and obey them. After Adam (peace be upon him) a succession of Messengers and Prophets came to renew the Guidance of Allah which was either lost or had become mixed up with human intrusions. The last Messenger and Prophet was Muḥammad (peace be upon him). He completed the chain of Prophets and, thus, sealed the succession. The Holy Qur'ān and his teachings are preserved for humanity till the end of time. Thus, it is the duty of the Muslim *Ummah* to carry forward the task which Prophets used to perform. This noble task is to provide guidance to humanity throughout the world.

What should be our duty towards the Prophet (peace be upon him)? This is explained by the second part of the *Kalimah* (Article of Faith), *Ashhadu anna Muḥammadar rasūlullāh*. In this part we bear witness that Muḥammad is Allah's Messenger. What does this witnessing entail? Our Faith in the Prophet as the True Messenger of Allah requires that we unconditionally obey him. The Qur'ān orders us:

يَـٰٓأَيُّهَا ٱلَّذِينَ ءَامَنُوٓا۟ أَطِيعُوا۟ ٱللَّهَ وَأَطِيعُوا۟ ٱلرَّسُولَ ... ﴿٥٩﴾

O you who believe! Obey Allah and obey the Messenger.

(al-Nisā' 4: 59)

وَمَآ أَرۡسَلۡنَا مِن رَّسُولٍ إِلَّا لِيُطَاعَ بِإِذۡنِ ٱللَّهِۚ ... ﴿٦٤﴾

We sent not a Messenger but to be obeyed, in accordance with the Will of Allah.

(al-Nisā' 4: 64)

These verses define the status of the Messenger as a Legislator and a Judge. In the very next verse of *Sūrah al-Nisā'* Allah (*swt*) says:

> *But no, by the Lord, they can have no (real) Faith until they make you judge in all disputes between them and find in their souls no resistance against your decisions, but accept them with fullest conviction.*

It is not only obedience that is required but we are told to follow the Messenger step by step (*Ittibā'*). The Qur'ān advises us:

قُلۡ إِن كُنتُمۡ تُحِبُّونَ ٱللَّهَ فَٱتَّبِعُونِي يُحۡبِبۡكُمُ ٱللَّهُ وَيَغۡفِرۡ
لَكُمۡ ذُنُوبَكُمۡۚ وَٱللَّهُ غَفُورٞ رَّحِيمٞ ﴿٣١﴾

Say: "If you do love Allah, follow me: Allah will love you and forgive your sins; for Allah is Oft Forgiving, Most Merciful."

(Āl 'Imrān 3: 31)

Obedience and following the Prophet may be seen as a legal requirement. We may obey the laws and follow regulations but in our hearts we do not agree with them and might even hate them. But our *Īmān* for the Prophet requires the utmost respect for and love of the Prophet (peace be upon him). Our *Īmān* is not complete and reliable until we love the Prophet more than anyone else. The Prophet (peace be upon him) is reported to have said:

لاَ يُؤْمِنُ أَحَدُكُمْ حَتَّى أَكُـونَ أَحَـبَّ إِلَيْهِ مِنْ وَالِدِهِ وَوَلَدِهِ
وَالنَّاسِ أَجْمَعِينَ

(متفق عليه)

> You cannot be a *Mu'min* unless you love me more than yourself, your father and your sons and all other human beings.
>
> (Bukhārī and Muslim)

Thus, our relationship with the Prophet is of intense love, respect and honour. To fulfil our obligations to our beloved Prophet we have to follow the *Sunnah* of the Prophet in our lives. There are very many instances from the life of the Companions that their love and devotion for the Prophet was unprecedented. Once a Companion and his son came to meet the Prophet and saw that the top button of his shirt was undone. They went back to their village and always left the top button of their shirts undone. It is reported of Bayazīd Bustāmī (may Allah have mercy on him), an eminently pious person, that he refused to eat water melon and said he did not know whether the Prophet had eaten this fruit and if he had then how did he eat it. These are extreme examples of the attachment that Companions and pious persons displayed to the *Sunnah* of the Prophet (peace be upon him).

Let us pray that Allah may strengthen our *Īmān* and guide us to obey Him and His Prophet with love and sincerity. (*Āmīn.*)

Ākhirah

يَـٰٓأَيُّهَا ٱلنَّاسُ ٱتَّقُوا۟ رَبَّكُمْ ۚ إِنَّ زَلْزَلَةَ ٱلسَّاعَةِ شَىْءٌ عَظِيمٌ ﴿١﴾

O mankind! Fear your Lord! For the convulsion of the Hour (of Judgement) will be a thing terrible.
(al-Ḥajj 22: 1)

Belief in Life after Death has always been a basic teaching of all the Prophets. Without this belief, life on this earth does not make much sense. We see very many injustices and wrongs being done all around us. The perpetrators of such crimes are not always caught nor are they sufficiently punished to fit the crime they committed. Then there are many pious people who selflessly devote their lives to doing good deeds. They are not always rewarded for their good deeds. This does not seem very fair. Hence, if we do not believe in Life after Death, where people will be punished and rewarded properly for their deeds, all other beliefs become meaningless.

Similarly, if a man does not believe in the Day of Judgement and does not think that he is accountable for his deeds, then he can pursue a life of pleasure and wickedness. There will be no incentive for him to follow the Code of Life provided by Allah and His Messenger. Why should he undergo trials and tribulations and suffer hardships? Unlike the one who does not believe in the Day of Judgement is the one who is cautious in his life and who acts according to dictates of the *Sharī'ah*. He will always remember that he is accountable to Allah for his deeds. He will know that he will face the consequences for his actions in this world and in the Hereafter. Thus, he will lead a life of piety and righteousness. Thus, this belief has a radical effect on people's lives.

As we believe that our Creator is *Ḥakīm* (Wise), *'Ādil* (Just) and *Raḥīm* (Merciful), then it is logical that He would not treat His obedient and pious servants the same way as wicked and evil people. Thus, in *Sūrah al-Fātiḥah* Allah's attributes of Mercy are followed by "Master of the Day of Judgement," and in *Sūrah al-Ḥijr*, there is a juxtaposition of Allah's Mercy and His Judgement:

نَبِّئْ عِبَادِيٓ أَنِّيٓ أَنَا ٱلْغَفُورُ ٱلرَّحِيمُ ﴿٤٩﴾ وَأَنَّ عَذَابِي هُوَ ٱلْعَذَابُ ٱلْأَلِيمُ ﴿٥٠﴾

Tell My servants that I am indeed the Oft-Forgiving, Most Merciful • And My Penalty will be indeed the most grievous Penalty.

(al-Ḥijr 15: 49–50)

In every age, people have raised doubts about Life after Death. The Holy Qur'ān has recorded their doubts in several places:

وَقَالُوٓاْ أَءِذَا ضَلَلْنَا فِي ٱلْأَرْضِ أَءِنَّا لَفِي خَلْقٍ جَدِيدٍۭ ۚ بَلْ هُم بِلِقَآءِ رَبِّهِمْ كَٰفِرُونَ ﴿١٠﴾

And they say: "What! When we lie hidden and lost, in the earth, shall we indeed be in a Creation renewed?" Nay, they deny the meeting with their Lord!.

(al-Sajdah 32: 10)

أَءِذَا مِتْنَا وَكُنَّا تُرَابًا ۖ ذَٰلِكَ رَجْعٌۢ بَعِيدٌ ﴿٣﴾

What! When we die and become dust (shall we live again?). That is a (sort of) return far (from our understanding).

(Qāf 50: 3)

وَقَالُوٓاْ أَءِذَا كُنَّا عِظَٰمًا وَرُفَٰتًا أَءِنَّا لَمَبْعُوثُونَ خَلْقًا جَدِيدًا ﴿٤٩﴾

They say: "What! When we are reduced to bones and dust, should we really be raised up (to be) a new creation?"

(al-Isrā' 17: 49)

The Qur'ān has drawn the attention of these doubters to Creation itself. If you believe that Allah has created the Heavens and the Earth and all what they contain, then is it beyond belief that He cannot re-create you?

ءَأَنتُمْ أَشَدُّ خَلْقًا أَمِ ٱلسَّمَآءُ ۚ بَنَىٰهَا ﴿٢٧﴾

What! Are you more difficult to create or the Heaven (above) Allah has constructed?

(al-Nāzi'āt 79: 27)

أَوَلَمْ يَرَوْا۟ أَنَّ ٱللَّهَ ٱلَّذِى خَلَقَ ٱلسَّمَٰوَٰتِ وَٱلْأَرْضَ قَادِرٌ
عَلَىٰٓ أَن يَخْلُقَ مِثْلَهُمْ ... ﴿٩٩﴾

See they not that Allah Who created the Heavens and the earth, has power to create the like of them (anew)?

(al-Isrā' 17: 99)

The other argument used is the revival of dead earth by rain. This is a common observance whereby after a long period of drought a shower of rain brings forth greenery:

وَأَحْيَيْنَا بِهِۦ بَلْدَةً مَّيْتًا ۚ كَذَٰلِكَ ٱلْخُرُوجُ ﴿١١﴾

We give (new) life therewith to land that is dead: thus will be the Resurrection.

(Qāf 50: 11)

قُلْ سِيرُوا۟ فِى ٱلْأَرْضِ فَٱنظُرُوا۟ كَيْفَ بَدَأَ ٱلْخَلْقَ ۚ ثُمَّ ٱللَّهُ يُنشِئُ
ٱلنَّشْأَةَ ٱلْءَاخِرَةَ ۚ إِنَّ ٱللَّهَ عَلَىٰ كُلِّ شَىْءٍ قَدِيرٌ ﴿٢٠﴾

Say: "Travel through the earth and see how Allah did originate creation; so will Allah produce a later creation: for Allah has power over all things."

(al-'Ankabūt 29: 20)

وَءَايَةٌ لَّهُمُ ٱلْأَرْضُ ٱلْمَيْتَةُ أَحْيَيْنَٰهَا وَأَخْرَجْنَا مِنْهَا
حَبًّا فَمِنْهُ يَأْكُلُونَ ﴿٣٣﴾

A Sign for them is the earth that is dead. We do give it life, and produce grain therefrom, of which you do eat.

(Yā Sīn 36: 33)

وَهُوَ ٱلَّذِى يُرْسِلُ ٱلرِّيَٰحَ بُشْرًۢا بَيْنَ يَدَىْ رَحْمَتِهِۦ ۖ حَتَّىٰٓ إِذَآ أَقَلَّتْ
سَحَابًا ثِقَالًا سُقْنَٰهُ لِبَلَدٍ مَّيِّتٍ فَأَنزَلْنَا بِهِ ٱلْمَآءَ فَأَخْرَجْنَا بِهِۦ مِن
كُلِّ ٱلثَّمَرَٰتِ ۚ كَذَٰلِكَ نُخْرِجُ ٱلْمَوْتَىٰ لَعَلَّكُمْ تَذَكَّرُونَ ﴿٥٧﴾

It is He Who sends the winds like heralds of glad tidings, going before His Mercy: when they have carried the heavy-laden clouds, We drive them to a land that is dead, make rain to descend thereon, and produce every kind of harvest therewith: thus shall We raise up the dead: perchance you may remember.

(al-Aʿrāf 7: 57)

وَٱللَّهُ ٱلَّذِىٓ أَرْسَلَ ٱلرِّيَٰحَ فَتُثِيرُ سَحَابًا فَسُقْنَٰهُ إِلَىٰ بَلَدٍ مَّيِّتٍ فَأَحْيَيْنَا
بِهِ ٱلْأَرْضَ بَعْدَ مَوْتِهَا ۚ كَذَٰلِكَ ٱلنُّشُورُ ﴿٩﴾

It is Allah Who sends forth the winds, so that they raise up the clouds and We drive them to a land that is dead, and revive the earth therewith after its death: even so (will be) the Resurrection!

(Fāṭir 35: 9)

The Holy Qur'ān argues on its premise on basic beliefs, using common observations in the life of common folk and does not rely on philosophical and metaphysical arguments which are beyond the reach of ordinary human beings.

The other line of argument is self-reflection. If a person were to reflect on how he was created, he would observe that life started as a humble drop of semen that grows in the womb. All constituents of his body are ordinary particles from the earth. The one who gave life first can re-create. Is this something hard to understand!

يَـٰٓأَيُّهَا ٱلنَّاسُ إِن كُنتُمْ فِى رَيْبٍ مِّنَ ٱلْبَعْثِ فَإِنَّا خَلَقْنَـٰكُم مِّن تُرَابٍ ثُمَّ
مِن نُّطْفَةٍ ثُمَّ مِنْ عَلَقَةٍ ثُمَّ مِن مُّضْغَةٍ مُّخَلَّقَةٍ وَغَيْرِ مُخَلَّقَةٍ لِّنُبَيِّنَ لَكُمْ ۚ
وَنُقِرُّ فِى ٱلْأَرْحَامِ مَا نَشَآءُ إِلَىٰٓ أَجَلٍ مُّسَمًّى ثُمَّ نُخْرِجُكُمْ طِفْلًا ثُمَّ
لِتَبْلُغُوٓا۟ أَشُدَّكُمْ ۖ وَمِنكُم مَّن يُتَوَفَّىٰ وَمِنكُم مَّن يُرَدُّ إِلَىٰٓ أَرْذَلِ
ٱلْعُمُرِ لِكَيْلَا يَعْلَمَ مِنۢ بَعْدِ عِلْمٍ شَيْـًٔا ۚ وَتَرَى ٱلْأَرْضَ هَامِدَةً
فَإِذَآ أَنزَلْنَا عَلَيْهَا ٱلْمَآءَ ٱهْتَزَّتْ وَرَبَتْ وَأَنۢبَتَتْ مِن كُلِّ زَوْجٍۭ
بَهِيجٍ ﴿٥﴾ ذَٰلِكَ بِأَنَّ ٱللَّهَ هُوَ ٱلْحَقُّ وَأَنَّهُۥ يُحْىِ ٱلْمَوْتَىٰ وَأَنَّهُۥ
عَلَىٰ كُلِّ شَىْءٍ قَدِيرٌ ﴿٦﴾

O mankind! If you have doubt about the Resurrection, (consider) that We created you out of dust, then out of sperm, then out of a leech-like clot, then out of a morsel of flesh, partly formed and partly unformed, in order that We may manifest (Our Power) to you; and We cause whom We will to rest in the wombs for an appointed term, then do We bring you out as babes, then you may reach your age of full strength; and some of you are called to die, and some are sent back to the feeblest old age, so that they know nothing after having known (much) and (further) you see the earth barren and lifeless but when We pour down rain on it; it is stirred (to life) it swells, and it puts forth every kind of beautiful growth in

pairs, this is so, because Allah is the Reality. It is
He Who gives life to the dead and it is He
Who has power over all things.

(al-Ḥajj 22: 5–6).

It is worth remembering that the Hereafter will be different from this world. There will be metamorphoses and radical changes in everything. Material things will lose their weight and actions and deeds will have weight and can be measured. Reality of everything will be revealed. Inanimate objects and parts of the human body will be able to speak! Thus, there is no escape from that Day, when the whole of mankind will be assembled and each one has to give account of his deeds individually before Allah (*swt*). There will be no one to help and to intercede on his behalf. Each one will be asked to recite his own record and judge for himself. There are many verses that graphically depict the Day of Judgement. Even the very many graphic words used for that Day are indicative of its horror and its calamity. Some of these words are:

al-Qāriʿah	The Calamity
al-Zalzalah	The Earthquake
al-Ḥāqqah	The Reality
al-Ṭāmmatul Kubrā	The Great Disaster
al-Ṣāʿiqah	The Blast
Yawman Thaqīlā	The Hard Day
Yawm al-Muḥīṭ	The Encompassing Day
Yawm al-Faṣl	The Day of Separation.

Some people are lulled into believing that the Day of Judgement is a longway away. There is no need to worry about it now. Yet the time for action is very short. We do not know when Death will overtake us. As soon as we die our time is up and we have to be ready to face our Lord. It is related that ʿUthmān ibn ʿAffān (may Allah be pleased with him) used to cry a lot when visiting the graveyard. People asked him the reason for this and he replied that the Prophet (peace be upon him) said:

إِنَّ الْقَبْرَ أَوَّلُ مَنْزِلٍ مِنْ مَنَازِلِ الآخِرَةِ فَإِنْ نَجَا مِنْهُ فَمَا بَعْدَهُ أَيْسَرُ مِنْهُ وَإِنْ لَمْ يَنْجُ مِنْهُ فَمَا بَعْدَهُ أَشَدُّ

(الترمذي وابن ماجة)

"The grave is the first of the stages of the *Ākhirah*. The one who attains salvation here, the rest of the journey will be easy. If he cannot attain salvation at this stage the rest of his journey will be more difficult and arduous."

(Tirmidhī and Ibn Mājah)

We should prepare ourselves for this journey now by good actions and good deeds.

May Allah keep us steadfast in our *Īmān* throughout our life so that we die in a state of *Īmān*. (*Āmīn*.)

Ṣalāh

إِنَّنِيٓ أَنَا ٱللَّهُ لَآ إِلَٰهَ إِلَّآ أَنَا۠ فَٱعۡبُدۡنِي وَأَقِمِ ٱلصَّلَوٰةَ لِذِكۡرِيٓ ﴿١٤﴾

Verily, I am Allah: There is no god but I: So you serve Me Alone. And establish regular Prayer for celebrating My praise.
(Ṭā Hā 20: 14)

A human being is primarily an *ʿAbd* – servant and slave. Hence, it is in his nature to worship his Creator and fulfil his covenant with God. To solidify this concept in the hearts and minds of people, Allah the Almighty has made *Ṣalāh* compulsory. To establish *Ṣalāh* is to remain with the natural religion of man.

The primary call of the Holy Qur'ān to human beings is to submit to their Creator. The manifestation of this submission is through *ʿIbādah* which means worship and obedience. This call for submission is proclaimed in many places in the Holy Qur'ān:

يَـٰٓأَيُّهَا ٱلنَّاسُ ٱعۡبُدُواْ رَبَّكُمُ ٱلَّذِي خَلَقَكُمۡ وَٱلَّذِينَ
مِن قَبۡلِكُمۡ لَعَلَّكُمۡ تَتَّقُونَ ﴿٢١﴾

O you people! Serve your Lord Who has created you as well as those before you, that you may become righteous.
(al-Baqarah 2: 21)

وَمَا خَلَقۡتُ ٱلۡجِنَّ وَٱلۡإِنسَ إِلَّا لِيَعۡبُدُونِ ﴿٥٦﴾

I have not created jinn *and mankind except to serve Me.*
(al-Dhāriyāt 51: 56)

وَلَقَدْ بَعَثْنَا فِى كُلِّ أُمَّةٍ رَّسُولًا أَنِ ٱعْبُدُوا۟ ٱللَّهَ
وَٱجْتَنِبُوا۟ ٱلطَّٰغُوتَ ... ﴿٣٦﴾

For We assuredly sent among every people a Messenger (with the command) Serve Allah, and avoid evil.

(al-Naḥl 16: 36)

The purpose of *Ṣalāh* is to establish an intimate relationship between the servant and his Creator. This is renewed five times a day and it continues throughout one's life. Thus, it creates a very intimate bond with the Creator. Unlike other acts of worship such as fasting, *Ḥajj* or *Zakāh*, which are required to be performed at specific times once a year, *Ṣalāh* is to be performed in all circumstances even when a person is ill or travelling. Again, in other acts of worship a person can do other things, for example a person can eat and drink during *Ḥajj* or buy and sell during fasting. But while praying no other task can be performed however small. The most complete concentration is essential when we are performing *Ṣalāh*. If we reflect, we will see that *Ṣalāh* is the embodiment of all *ʿIbādah*. For example, in *Ḥajj* we are required to visit the Kaʿbah and do *Ṭawāf*, in *Ṣalāh* we are required to face the direction of the Kaʿbah. In Ramaḍān during fasting we refrain from eating or drinking, similarly we are not allowed these acts while praying. *Zakāh* is the sacrifice of wealth while *Ṣalāh* is the sacrifice of time.

Ṣalāh is the most important obligation for a Muslim. After saying *Shahādah* by which we enter the fold of Islam, the very first obligation testing our sincerity is *Ṣalāh*. It is not only for this *Ummah* that *Ṣalāh* was made obligatory. But we read in the Holy Qur'ān that Allah (*swt*) enjoined the performance of *Ṣalāh* to the *Ummah* of all Prophets.

Again its importance can be judged by the fact that it is the only *ʿIbādah* which is made compulsory directly by Allah talking to the Prophet (peace be upon him) during *Miʿrāj*. It is mentioned in the *ḥadīth* that on the Day of Judgement the very first question asked by Allah will be about the performance of regular *Ṣalāh*. *Ṣalāh* plays a very important role in our lives as it brings us into direct communion with Allah, our Creator. Its neglect has dire consequences for us in the Hereafter. Its neglect will lead us into Hell-Fire. In *Sūrah al-Muddaththir* a conversation is narrated in which the sinners will be asked:

مَا سَلَكَكُمْ فِي سَقَرَ ﴿٤٢﴾ قَالُوا۟ لَمْ نَكُ مِنَ ٱلْمُصَلِّينَ ﴿٤٣﴾

"What led you into Hell-Fire?" They will say: "We were not of those who prayed."
(al-Muddaththir 74: 42–3)

The help of Allah is promised for those who perform Prayer. Thus, it is mentioned in the Holy Qur'ān:

وَقَالَ ٱللَّهُ إِنِّى مَعَكُمْ ۖ لَئِنْ أَقَمْتُمُ ٱلصَّلَوٰةَ

And Allah said: "I am with you if you establish regular Prayer."
(al-Mā'idah 5: 12)

Ṣalāh is the supreme act of submission by human beings before their Lord. When we bow down and prostrate we show our humility. Thus, it is the perfect embodiment of Allah's superiority and man's humbleness. In Prayer we establish a very close relationship with Allah. Indeed, we are nearest to Him when we are in prostration:

كَلَّا لَا تُطِعْهُ وَٱسْجُدْ وَٱقْتَرِب ۩ ﴿١٩﴾

Nay, heed him not; bow down in adoration and bring yourself closer (to Allah).
(al-'Alaq 96: 19)

It is narrated in the *aḥādīth* that by performing *Wuḍū'* and saying Prayers we wipe out minor sins and regular Prayer brings us into the presence of our Creator frequently. Hence we try to be cautious not to commit acts of indecency and immorality. This characteristic of *Ṣalāh* is mentioned in *Sūrah al-'Ankabūt*:

وَأَقِمِ ٱلصَّلَوٰةَ ۖ إِنَّ ٱلصَّلَوٰةَ تَنْهَىٰ عَنِ ٱلْفَحْشَآءِ وَٱلْمُنكَرِ ۗ

And establish regular Prayer: for Prayer restrains from shameful and unjust deeds.

(al-ʿAnkabūt 29: 45)

We are encouraged to pray in the Mosque and in congregation. Its reward is 27 times more than praying alone. This collective worship strengthens bonds of brotherhood among Muslims. When praying in the Mosque, we all stand in a row, shoulder to shoulder, rich and poor, the black and white of all nationalities, and this demonstrates the equality of all human beings.

Ṣalāh is really an intimate conversation with our Creator. Being a conversation, it is not a monologue. We read *Sūrah al-Fātiḥah* in every *Rakʿah*. In a *ḥadīth qudsī,* the Prophet relates from Allah how He responds to what we say:

قَسَمْتُ الصَّلَاةَ بَيْنِي وَبَيْنَ عَبْدِي نِصْفَيْنِ وَلِعَبْدِي مَا سَأَلَ فَإِذَا قَالَ الْعَبْدُ الْحَمْدُ لِلَّهِ رَبِّ الْعَالَمِينَ قَالَ اللَّهُ تَعَالَى حَمِدَنِي عَبْدِي وَإِذَا قَالَ الرَّحْمَنِ الرَّحِيمِ قَالَ اللَّهُ تَعَالَى أَثْنَى عَلَيَّ عَبْدِي وَإِذَا قَالَ مَالِكِ يَوْمِ الدِّينِ قَالَ مَجَّدَنِي عَبْدِي وَقَالَ مَرَّةً فَوَّضَ إِلَيَّ عَبْدِي فَإِذَا قَالَ إِيَّاكَ نَعْبُدُ وَإِيَّاكَ نَسْتَعِينُ قَالَ هَذَا بَيْنِي وَبَيْنَ عَبْدِي وَلِعَبْدِي مَا سَأَلَ فَإِذَا قَالَ اهْدِنَا الصِّرَاطَ الْمُسْتَقِيمَ صِرَاطَ الَّذِينَ أَنْعَمْتَ عَلَيْهِمْ غَيْرِ الْمَغْضُوبِ عَلَيْهِمْ وَلَا الضَّالِّينَ قَالَ هَذَا لِعَبْدِي وَلِعَبْدِي مَا سَأَلَ

(مسلم والترمذي واحمد)

I have divided the Prayer (*Ṣalāh*) between Me and My servant, half is for Me and half for him, and My servant shall have what he asked for. For when my servant says: "All praise belongs to God, the Lord of all the worlds", God says: "My servant has thanked Me and praised Me." When the servant

> says: "The Most Merciful, the Beneficent", Allah says: "My servant has extolled Me." When the servant says: "Master of the Day of Judgement", Allah says: "My servant has glorified Me... This is My portion." When he says: "You alone we worship and from You alone we seek help", Allah says: "This is common between My servant and Me. He will be given what he will ask." When he says: "Guide us on the Straight Path..." Allah says: "This belongs to My servant, and My servant shall have what he has asked for."
>
> (Muslim, Tirmidhī, Aḥmad)

We say two very great *Tasbīḥ* in *rukū'* and *sujūd.* We constantly praise and glorify and proclaim Allah's greatness. In *Tashahhud* and *Ṣalawāt* we praise Allah and seek His blessing upon the Prophet and his family. And finally in *Du'ā' al-Qunūt,* at night, we supplicate Allah and seek His special help.

Thus, in the short time we spend in each Prayer we converse with Allah and seek His Guidance and help in all our affairs. Prayer thus fulfils our spiritual as well as material needs. It is only through the blessings of Allah that we can survive in this world.

Let us pray that Allah may keep us steadfast in our *Īmān* and that we regularly pray and enrich our souls with love of Allah. (*Āmīn.*)

Ṣalāh: How to Make it Effective

ٱتْلُ مَآ أُوحِىَ إِلَيْكَ مِنَ ٱلْكِتَٰبِ وَأَقِمِ ٱلصَّلَوٰةَ ۖ إِنَّ ٱلصَّلَوٰةَ
تَنْهَىٰ عَنِ ٱلْفَحْشَآءِ وَٱلْمُنكَرِ ۗ ... ﴿٤٥﴾

Recite what is sent of the Book by revelation to you, and establish regular Prayer: for Prayer restrains from shameful and unjust deeds.

(al-'Ankabūt 29: 45)

We have discussed and explored so many benefits of Prayer yet we do not see their manifestation in our lives or in society at large. *Ṣalāh* does not seem to be effective for us. *Ṣalāh* is not effective precisely because our performance of *Ṣalāh* is not as it ought to be. Blessings from Prayer can only be acquired if we perform them as they should be performed. You may well ask: "What do you mean by this?" Let me explain: there are two aspects of our Prayer:

One is its outward appearance, the physical nature of our standing, bowing and prostrating. These are physical aspects of the Prayer. Then there is its intrinsic aspect. As we know every body has a soul. If there is no Soul the Body is useless. Thus, if there is no soul in our *Ṣalāh* it will be of no use to us. If there is a Soul in it, it will ascend higher and higher and its blessings will manifest in our lives and in our society.

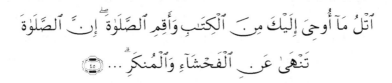

We must, therefore, reflect on this issue and consider how we can achieve effectiveness in our *Ṣalāh*. Firstly we have to create the psychological atmosphere for Prayer. This means our external environment must be such as to be conducive to tranquillity and peacefulness. This gives emphasis to what we are going to undertake, which is a very important task. Regulations laid down for the performance of *Ṣalāh* help to create this suitable psychological atmosphere in the following three phases:

First is our own preparation, which should be undertaken before *Ṣalāh*. It is essential that our body and clothes be clean. This is of course the precondition for *Ṣalāh*. Cleanliness of body and clothing ensures we are conscious of the important task we are going to perform. Then we are required to make *Wuḍū'* properly so that we are fresh and do not feel tired or sleepy. It is also essential that we select the place of worship, one which is quiet, and clean. Thus, the best place is the mosque where there are no distractions and *Ṣalāh* can be performed with full concentration. Therefore, there is great reward for performing *Ṣalāh* in a mosque. It is recommended that we perform two *Rak'ah Nafl* Prayers before sitting down in the mosque. This helps us to prepare for obligatory Prayers. Waiting for the start of the obligatory Prayers gives us time to become mentally prepared. While we are waiting for *Ṣalāh* it will focus our minds if we engage in *Dhikr* instead of sitting idly.

Our second preparation for *Ṣalāh* requires us to listen carefully to the Call for Prayer (*Adhān*) and after each sentence that the *Mu'adhdhin* says you should repeat it and answer it appropriately. At the end of *Adhān* pray to Allah (*swt*) to shower His blessings on the Prophet, his family and his Companions. Usually there are *Sunnah* Prayers preceding the obligatory Prayers. You should pray the appropriate number of *Rak'ah*. When *Iqāmah* is said it is essential to stand up shoulder to shoulder, and fill the gaps and straighten the rows and get ready for the Prayer.

Finally, during the Prayers it is essential that we should try to concentrate and listen attentively to what the *Imām* is reciting. When the *Imām* is not reciting aloud, then remember Allah silently. It will help our concentration if we realise that we are standing in the presence of our Lord and we are really *seeing* our Lord. If this is difficult to imagine, then at least we should feel that Our Lord is *seeing* us. This is the status of *Aḥsan* (excellence) which is mentioned in the *ḥadīth*. The conscious realisation that our Lord is observing us will create a feeling of humility, lowliness, and extreme submissiveness before the Holy of the Holiest, Supreme, High, Lofty and our Creator. Allah promises success and salvation for:

ٱلَّذِينَ هُمْ فِى صَلَاتِهِمْ خَـٰشِعُونَ ۝٢

Those who humble themselves in their Prayers.
(al-Mu'minūn 23: 2)

This will generate a feeling of complete devotion, love and adoration for our Lord. It is essential that we should earnestly pledge to improve ourselves and to do better in the performance of our Prayers as success is guaranteed for:

وَٱلَّذِينَ هُمْ عَلَىٰ صَلَوَٰتِهِمْ يُحَافِظُونَ ۝٩

Those who (strictly) guard their Prayers.
(al-Mu'minūn 23: 9)

Thus if we try to listen and understand what is being recited by the *Imām* and reflect on its meaning, this will help us to concentrate in our Prayers. Do not be in a rush to get out of the mosque after finishing Prayers. We should have time to sit and reflect and do some *Dhikr* and *Tasbīḥ* before engaging ourselves in our daily chores.

Thus, for making our *Ṣalāh* effective we should make a start by first having the firm intention and complete determination that we will try our best to perform our Prayers properly. It will help us enormously if we try to learn the meanings of all that we read in our *Ṣalāh*. This will help us to concentrate our minds on what is being read instead of wandering and thinking about all manner of other things. Thus, when you raise your hands and say *Allāhu Akbar* and start the *Ṣalāh* assume that you are cutting yourself out of this world and transporting yourself to another world. You should relinquish all your worries about worldly affairs and concentrate your mind solely on your presence before your Lord.

Preparing yourself for the *Ṣalāh* and concentrating your mind during the *Ṣalāh* will surely make your *Ṣalāh* effective. Having said this it is also necessary to be aware of and to guard yourself against some pitfalls that can sometimes be encountered. Mawlānā Amīn Aḥsan Iṣlāḥī in his valuable book *Tazkiyah-e-Nafs* mentioned the following as most lethal:

Laziness is something that affects us all from time to time. Satan tries to lull us into forgetfulness. Thus, we sometimes fail to perform Prayers at the right time. As you know it is most important to pray at the proper time. Sometimes we also neglect to pray in *Jamā'ah.* Sometimes we are unable to concentrate because our minds are preoccupied with some pressing problem. Laziness may be due to feeling sleepy, tired or being busy. These are physical aspects of laziness and they can be overcome by determination and firm intention. But there is another kind of laziness, that is the sign of hypocrisy (*Nifāq*). This is much more serious. To cure *Nifāq* we should seek Allah's help. We should realise that Prayer is the most important pillar of Islam and it is the practical manifestation of our *Īmān*. By vitiating our Prayers we are endangering our Faith. To overcome these shortcomings the *'Ulamā'* have recommended that we should consciously train ourselves to obey Allah. Thus, we have to make Prayers part of our lives without which we should feel we cannot exist. Another step you should take is to have the firm determination to wake up in the morning and once you are out of bed you will drive away the Satan who is trying to prolong your stay in bed.

Another pitfall that we should be aware of is distraction (*Wasāwis.*) This includes distraction of mind, doubt, temptation, and worldly thought which keeps the mind wandering from one thing to the next. Often in Prayers you suddenly remember things that have been forgotten for a long time. This is due to Satan who tries to distract you from remembering Allah properly. To overcome this the *'Ulamā'* recommend that you should consciously say: "I take refuge of Allah from accursed Satan." You should not read silently but a bit aloud so that you can hear yourself. If you know what you are reading it will help to concentrate your mind. It is essential that you keep your thoughts clean. Thus, even if you are distracted you will still be thinking about good things and not bad and evil things. If, after all these efforts, you are still distracted then try to counter feelings of self-doubt by positively thinking about the Prayers. And finally if you try to understand the purpose of Prayer, that it is an act of submission to our Creator, surely Allah will help you.

The other serious pitfall is termed as stealing. It is surprising to mention stealing in Prayer, but, yes, it is stealing when we try to complete all the *Arkān* of *Ṣalāh* very quickly. When we rush through them to complete our Prayers as quickly as possible, this is robbing the sanctity of Prayers. We should try to perform all sections of Prayer, that is *Qiyām*, *Rukū'* and *Sujūd*, without undue haste, only then will we be saying our *Ṣalāh* properly.

The most deadly pitfall of all is *Riyā'* – an outward show of piety. It is one of the deadly sins. *Riyā'* means that we are performing Prayer so that others can see that we are very pious. Thus, it is *Ṣalāh* for the sake of others. This is of course a grave sin. It is a form of *Shirk*. Hence, we should all take extreme and stringent steps to rid ourselves of these feelings. Allah will never accept such Prayers and instead of reward we will be attracting His wrath.

Let us pray that Allah may accept our Prayers, make them effective and protect us from all the pitfalls and temptations which vitiate our Prayers. (*Āmīn.*)

Infāq fī Sabīl Allāh

إِنَّ ٱلَّذِينَ يَتْلُونَ كِتَٰبَ ٱللَّهِ وَأَقَامُوا۟ ٱلصَّلَوٰةَ وَأَنفَقُوا۟ مِمَّا رَزَقْنَٰهُمْ
سِرًّا وَعَلَانِيَةً يَرْجُونَ تِجَٰرَةً لَّن تَبُورَ ﴿٢٩﴾

Those who recite the Book of Allah, establish regular Prayer, and spend something (in charity) both secretly and openly out of what We have provided for them, may hope for a business that never fails.

(Fāṭir 35: 29)

After Prayers the other most important commandment of Allah is *Zakāh*. Prayers are the acknowledgement of the right of the Creator to be worshipped and obeyed. *Zakāh* is meeting the need of fellow human beings. It is to provide help and welfare to those who are unable to meet their needs due to poverty, illness or disability.

The word *Zakāh* means purification, growth and development. It is significant to note that Islam uses this word for setting aside a portion of our wealth for helping the needy and poor in society. There is a tendency in us to save money or to spend on our own needs. This greediness and selfishness in us is purified by imposing on us a duty to give away money to others so that those who are unable to compete in the economic arena can be looked after and no one remains destitute in society. This act of purification is accomplished by giving *Zakāh* as well as other *Ṣadaqāt* in the way of Allah. Thus, the comprehensive term for charity is *Infāq fī Sabīl Allāh* (spending in the way of Allah). Whereas *Zakāh* is fixed at 2½ percent of our savings, to be paid every year, *Infāq* is a voluntary payment to be given whenever we can spare it after meeting our needs.

Ṣalāh and *Zakāh* are twin duties that all Prophets have commanded their followers to observe. Their neglect is the cause of eternal damnation as this conversation with those in Hell illustrates:

مَا سَلَكَكُمْ فِى سَقَرَ ﴿٤٢﴾ قَالُوا۟ لَمْ نَكُ مِنَ ٱلْمُصَلِّينَ ﴿٤٣﴾
وَلَمْ نَكُ نُطْعِمُ ٱلْمِسْكِينَ ﴿٤٤﴾

"What led you into Hell-Fire?" • They will say: "We were not of those who prayed • nor were we of those who fed the poor."
(al-Muddaththir 74: 42–4)

Allah (*swt*) urges believers to spend from their wealth so that they can save themselves from a grievous penalty:

يَـٰٓأَيُّهَا ٱلَّذِينَ ءَامَنُوٓا۟ أَنفِقُوا۟ مِمَّا رَزَقْنَـٰكُم مِّن قَبْلِ أَن يَأْتِىَ يَوْمٌ
لَّا بَيْعٌ فِيهِ وَلَا خُلَّةٌ وَلَا شَفَـٰعَةٌ ۗ

O you who believe! Spend out of (the bounties) We have provided for you, before the Day comes when no bargaining (will avail), nor friendship nor intercession.
(al-Baqarah 2: 254)

وَٱلَّذِينَ يَكْنِزُونَ ٱلذَّهَبَ وَٱلْفِضَّةَ وَلَا يُنفِقُونَهَا فِى سَبِيلِ ٱللَّهِ
فَبَشِّرْهُم بِعَذَابٍ أَلِيمٍ ﴿٣٤﴾ يَوْمَ يُحْمَىٰ عَلَيْهَا فِى نَارِ جَهَنَّمَ فَتُكْوَىٰ
بِهَا جِبَاهُهُمْ وَجُنُوبُهُمْ وَظُهُورُهُمْ ۖ هَـٰذَا مَا كَنَزْتُمْ لِأَنفُسِكُمْ
فَذُوقُوا۟ مَا كُنتُمْ تَكْنِزُونَ ﴿٣٥﴾

And there are those who accumulate gold and silver and spend not in the Way of Allah: announce them a most grievous penalty • On the Day when heat will be produced out of the (wealth) in the fire of Hell, and with it will be branded their foreheads, their flanks, and their backs – "This is the (treasure) which you hoarded for yourselves: taste you then, the (treasure) you buried."

(al-Tawbah 9: 34–5)

The reason being that excessive attachment to wealth is the root of all evil. A person never feels satisfied with what he has and tries to accumulate as much as possible for himself and his family whereas others in his neighbourhood are destitute and dying of hunger. Wealth that is given to an individual is a trust from Allah (*swt*) and it is His blessing. As all things in this Universe belong to Allah so does the wealth that is in the possession of human beings. Thus, it is instructive to note that Allah (*swt*) says in the Holy Qur'ān that the poor have a right to your wealth. So if you give others charity you are only fulfilling your duty as trustees handing back what already belongs to them:

وَفِيٓ أَمۡوَٰلِهِمۡ حَقّٞ لِّلسَّآئِلِ وَٱلۡمَحۡرُومِ ١٩

And in their wealth and possessions is a recognised right for the needy who ask, and for those who are deprived.

(al-Dhāriyāt 51: 19)

وَٱلَّذِينَ فِيٓ أَمۡوَٰلِهِمۡ حَقّٞ مَّعۡلُومٞ ٢٤ لِّلسَّآئِلِ وَٱلۡمَحۡرُومِ ٢٥

And those in whose wealth is a recognised right for the needy who ask • and for those who are deprived.

(al-Ma'ārij 70: 24–5)

Sometimes we give away things to charity which we want to discard, for example old clothes or furniture. This is not, however, a sign of our generosity. Unless we give away our wealth with a purity of heart and give away things which we love dearly we cannot achieve goodness. As the Qur'ān says:

يَـٰٓأَيُّهَا ٱلَّذِينَ ءَامَنُوٓا۟ أَنفِقُوا۟ مِن طَيِّبَـٰتِ مَا كَسَبْتُمْ وَمِمَّآ أَخْرَجْنَا
لَكُم مِّنَ ٱلْأَرْضِ ۖ وَلَا تَيَمَّمُوا۟ ٱلْخَبِيثَ مِنْهُ تُنفِقُونَ وَلَسْتُم
بِـَٔاخِذِيهِ إِلَّآ أَن تُغْمِضُوا۟ فِيهِ ۚ ... ﴿٢٦٧﴾

O you who believe! Give the good things that you have (honourably) earned, and the fruits of the earth which We have produced for you. And do not even contemplate at giving away anything that is bad such as you and yourselves would not accept or accept only by overlooking its defects.
(al-Baqarah 2: 267)

لَن تَنَالُوا۟ ٱلْبِرَّ حَتَّىٰ تُنفِقُوا۟ مِمَّا تُحِبُّونَ ۚ وَمَا تُنفِقُوا۟
مِن شَىْءٍ فَإِنَّ ٱللَّهَ بِهِۦ عَلِيمٌ ﴿٩٢﴾

By no means shall you attain righteousness unless you give (freely) of that which you love (in the way of Allah); Allah knows it well whatever you spend.
(Āl ʿImrān 3: 92)

It is narrated by Anas that Abū Ṭalḥah had the best orchard of dates and palms in Madinah in front of the Prophet's Mosque. The Prophet (peace be upon him) used to visit it and eat dates and drink sweet water from the well. When this *āyah* was revealed he came to the Prophet (peace be upon him) and said: "I now hand over my palm garden which I love very much in *Ṣadaqah* and you can dispose of it as you like." The Prophet (peace be upon him) said: "This is a very profitable garden. I have heard what you have said but my advice is for you to divide this among your relations." Abū Ṭalḥah did as directed by the Prophet (peace be upon him) and divided it among his near relations and cousins. How valuable this orchard was can be guessed from the fact that only one portion of the orchard that Ḥassān ibn Thābit received from Abū Ṭalḥah was later sold to Muʿāwiyah for a hundred thousand *dirhams*.

It is essential to take care not to vitiate our *ʿIbādah* by *Riyā'* (showing off). The intention should always be to help the poor or to feed the hungry for the sake of Allah (*swt*) and not to be known as generous:

وَيُطْعِمُونَ ٱلطَّعَامَ عَلَىٰ حُبِّهِۦ مِسْكِينًا وَيَتِيمًا وَأَسِيرًا ﴿٨﴾
إِنَّمَا نُطْعِمُكُمْ لِوَجْهِ ٱللَّهِ لَا نُرِيدُ مِنكُمْ جَزَآءً وَلَا شُكُورًا ﴿٩﴾

And they feed, for the love of Allah, the needy, the orphan, and the captive • (Saying): "We feed you for the sake of Allah alone: no reward do we desire from you, or thanks."
(al-Dahr 76: 8–9)

ٱلَّذِى يُؤْتِى مَالَهُۥ يَتَزَكَّىٰ ﴿١٨﴾ وَمَا لِأَحَدٍ عِندَهُۥ مِن نِّعْمَةٍ تُجْزَىٰٓ ﴿١٩﴾
إِلَّا ٱبْتِغَآءَ وَجْهِ رَبِّهِ ٱلْأَعْلَىٰ ﴿٢٠﴾ وَلَسَوْفَ يَرْضَىٰ ﴿٢١﴾

Those who spend their wealth for increase in self-purification • and have in their minds no favour from anyone for which a reward is expected in return • but only the desire to seek for the Countenance of their Lord, Most High • and soon will they attain (complete) satisfaction
(al-Layl 92: 18–21)

Again it is essential to treat people nicely even if we are not able to help them. Allah asks us:

وَأَمَّا ٱلسَّآئِلَ فَلَا تَنْهَرْ ﴿١٠﴾

Do not repulse the beggar.
(al-Ḍuḥā 93: 10)

Help and charity should be provided without offending its recipients:

ٱلَّذِينَ يُنفِقُونَ أَمْوَٰلَهُمْ فِى سَبِيلِ ٱللَّهِ ثُمَّ لَا يُتْبِعُونَ مَآ أَنفَقُوا۟
مَنًّا وَلَآ أَذًى ۙ لَّهُمْ أَجْرُهُمْ عِندَ رَبِّهِمْ وَلَا خَوْفٌ عَلَيْهِمْ وَلَا هُمْ
يَحْزَنُونَ ﴿٢٦٢﴾ قَوْلٌ مَّعْرُوفٌ وَمَغْفِرَةٌ خَيْرٌ مِّن صَدَقَةٍ يَتْبَعُهَآ أَذًى ۗ
وَٱللَّهُ غَنِىٌّ حَلِيمٌ ﴿٢٦٣﴾ يَـٰٓأَيُّهَا ٱلَّذِينَ ءَامَنُوا۟ لَا تُبْطِلُوا۟ صَدَقَـٰتِكُم
بِٱلْمَنِّ وَٱلْأَذَىٰ كَٱلَّذِى يُنفِقُ مَالَهُۥ رِئَآءَ ٱلنَّاسِ ... ﴿٢٦٤﴾

Those who spend their wealth in the cause of Allah, and not undo their gifts with reminders of their generosity or with injury – for them their reward is with their Lord; on them shall be no fear nor shall they grieve. Kind words and covering of faults are better than charity followed by injury. Allah is free of all wants and He is most Forbearing • O you who believe! Cancel not your charity by reminders of your generosity or by injury – like those who spend their wealth to be seen by people…

(al-Baqarah 2: 262–4)

Thus, the purpose of *Zakāh* and *Ṣadaqāt* is to purify us and to create a close relationship with Allah and His Creation. It disperses the wealth in society and helps to create a just and caring society. The other purpose has to do with the propagation and expansion of the Message of Islam by winning peoples' hearts.

Let us pray that Allah (*swt*) may make us generous so that we spend our money for the welfare of humanity for His sake and for achieving salvation. (*Āmīn.*)

Ṣawm

يَـٰٓأَيُّهَا ٱلَّذِينَ ءَامَنُوا۟ كُتِبَ عَلَيْكُمُ ٱلصِّيَامُ كَمَا كُتِبَ عَلَى
ٱلَّذِينَ مِن قَبْلِكُمْ لَعَلَّكُمْ تَتَّقُونَ ﴿١٨٣﴾

O you who believe! Fasting is prescribed to you as it was prescribed to those before you that you may be God-Conscious.
(al-Baqarah 2: 183)

The blessed month of Ramaḍān in which Allah (*swt*) has prescribed fasting is with us. The Arabic word for fasting is *Ṣawm.* It literally means to refrain from something or to leave something. The Arabs used to train their horses by refraining them from food. Hence this word now means refraining from food and drink. The purposes for which fasting is prescribed are to teach self-control and patience (*Ṣabr*) by breaking the grip of habit and to create *Taqwā* (God-Consciousness). Thus, by acquiring the qualities of *Ṣabr* and *Taqwā* a person is trained to withstand adverse situations. Fasting is of such fundamental importance that all religions have prescribed it on their followers.

As the prime purpose of fasting is *Taqwā,* let us explore its meaning. It is very difficult to translate it in one word. It is often translated as Fear, that is to refrain from doing wrong because of the fear of punishment. But it is much more than fear, hence God-Consciousness is the term that conveys a more comprehensive meaning. The best definition is provided by Kaʿb ibn Mālik (may Allah be pleased with him). ʿUmar ibn Khaṭṭāb (may Allah be pleased with him) once asked Kaʿb: "What is *Taqwā*?" He said:

"Have you ever traversed a narrow path which is covered with prickly bushes on either side?" 'Umar replied: "Yes, I have." Ka'b then asked: "How did you walk on this path?" 'Umar said: "I gathered together all my clothes very tightly around myself and walked very carefully." Ka'b said: "This is *Taqwā*." Thus, we have to go through this life very carefully avoiding all pitfalls and temptations.

Deeper study of the Holy Qur'ān shows that *Taqwā* is the purpose of all *'Ibādah* not only of fasting but also of *Ṣalāh, Zakāh, Ḥajj* and the Sacrifice of animals as well. The following verses indicate this:

Sūrah al-Baqarah, verse 177 enumerates many righteous deeds of the Truthful (*Ṣādiqīn*) and of the God-fearing (*Muttaqīn*). In this list are "those who establish Prayer and practise regular charity (*Zakāh*)." In the same *Sūrah*, verse 197 states:

وَتَزَوَّدُوا۟ فَإِنَّ خَيْرَ ٱلزَّادِ ٱلتَّقْوَىٰ ۚ ... ﴿١٩٧﴾

And take provision (with you) for the journey (of Ḥajj), but the best provision is Taqwā.

(al-Baqarah 2: 197)

In *Sūrah al-Ḥajj* Allah (*swt*) says:

لَن يَنَالَ ٱللَّهَ لُحُومُهَا وَلَا دِمَآؤُهَا وَلَٰكِن يَنَالُهُ
ٱلتَّقْوَىٰ مِنكُمْ ۚ ... ﴿٣٧﴾

It is neither their meat nor their blood that reaches Allah: it is your Taqwā that reaches Him.

(al-Ḥajj 22: 37)

Similarly, in all other aspects of our lives *Taqwā* is required. It may be in our dress, in retribution or justice but they all require God-Consciousness. Even Guidance from the Qur'ān is for those who are *Muttaqīn* (the pious ones) (*al-Baqarah* 2: 2).

Thus, the first call of all Prophets was:

إِنِّى لَكُمْ رَسُولٌ أَمِينٌ ﴿١٢٥﴾ فَٱتَّقُوا۟ ٱللَّهَ وَأَطِيعُونِ ﴿١٢٦﴾

"I am to you a Messenger worthy of trust • So fear Allah and obey me."

(al-Shu'arā' 26: 125–6)

Having seen the meaning of *Taqwā* and considered its importance, let us reflect on how fasting helps in creating God-Consciousness. The act of fasting is solely between an individual and his Creator. A person can pretend to fast and eat secretly and no one will know. Yet as all of us appreciate, Allah is overseeing us and watching all our deeds. Thus, fasting creates this constant awareness of Allah. Again fasting, unlike other acts of *'Ibādah*, is invisible to others, thus, it saves us from showing off our piety. Fasting creates *Taqwā* in our spirit and thought. Fasting also enables us to have self-control on all our desires such as hunger, thirst, sleep and sexual gratification.

Fasting is the mirror of the Islamic concept of *Taqwā*. Fasting gives us a very clear interpretation of the Islamic personality. The concept of *Dīn* that Islam proclaims as the only way for the salvation of human beings is very well portrayed in fasting. This means that fasting not only makes a person *Muttaqī* in his behaviour but also in his outlook and thought. Fasting provides a very comprehensive training for *Taqwā* and produces a well-rounded personality. Sometimes people become so obsessed with piety that they want to outdo others by inflicting more hardship on themselves than what is required by *Sharī'ah*. The following *aḥādīth* of the Prophet (peace be upon him) will illustrate this point:

لاَ صِيامَ لِمَنْ صَامَ الدَّهْرَ

(البخاري)

One who fasted throughout (i.e. without any break) has not fasted at all.

(Bukhārī)

نَهَى رَسُولُ اللَّهِ صَلَّى اللَّهُ عَلَيْهِ وَسَلَّمَ عَنْ الْوِصَالِ فِي الصَّوْمِ

(مسلم)

The Prophet (peace be upon him) prohibited against joining two fasts (i.e. fasting without *Suḥūr*).

(Muslim)

لَيْسَ مِنْ الْبِرِّ الصَّوْمُ فِي السَّفَرِ

(متفق عليه)

It is not a good deed to fast during travel.

(Bukhārī and Muslim)

These *aḥādīth* give a different interpretation of piety. *Taqwā* and piety do not mean that we have to torture ourselves. The requirement is rather to exercise self-control.

Fasting not only creates *Taqwā* but also gives real meaning to piety. These aspects of piety are usually not properly understood. When we speak of a *Muttaqī* we think of someone who is very strong in tempering his soul. But Islam requires *Taqwā* that helps a person to keep control of his carnal self (*Nafs al-Ammārah*) and to stop him from transgressing the bounds of the *Sharī'ah*. It does not mean that one should torture oneself in such a way as to reduce one's power and capability to be effective. In other religions, such excesses of piety led many of their followers astray. Regulations with respect to fasting remind us to be moderate and to refrain from being over-zealous. Several *aḥādīth* in addition to the ones quoted above bring out this message very clearly:

تَسَحَّرُوا فَإِنَّ فِي السُّحُورِ بَرَكَةً

(متفق عليه)

Have *Suḥūr* (early morning meal), as there is *Barakah* in *Suḥūr*.

(Bukhārī and Muslim)

لاَ يَزَالُ النَّاسُ بِخَيْرٍ مَا عَجَّلُوا الْفِطْرَ

(متفق عليه)

People will remain in blessing until they do *Ifṭār* (break their fasts) promptly.

(Bukhārī and Muslim)

لاَ يَزَالُ الدِّينُ ظَاهِرًا مَا عَجَّلَ النَّاسُ الْفِطْرَ

(أبو داود)

Dīn will remain dominant until people do *Ifṭār* promptly.
(Abū Dā'ūd)

قَالَ اللّٰهُ عَزَّ وَجَلَّ أَحَبُّ عِبَادِي إِلَيَّ أَعْجَلُهُمْ فِطْرًا

(الترمذي)

Allah says: "My most beloved servant is one who breaks his fast promptly.
(Tirmidhī)

These *aḥādīth* instruct us to avoid excesses and not to torture ourselves. They also indicate what is meant by self-control. This control means control of our opinions and our tastes as well. Just as we are required to follow the injunctions of Allah in fasting and to refrain from food, drink and sex during the hours of fasting, we also have to have control over our opinions, inclinations and tastes. These too should be subservient to Allah's will.

As human beings, we are creatures of habit. For example, the routine of our daily work, helps us to organise our lives systematically. Yet at times we become slaves of such self-imposed habits. Any change in our routine upsets us. If we do not have our coffee break at 11, we feel distraught. Thus, instead of our lives being regulated by us we become slaves to our habits. Fasting brings about a complete change in our daily routine. We eat and drink at different times, our schedule of sleep and rest is changed. Instead of being slaves to our habits and our desires we are given control over our own lives. This liberating feeling of being master of our own destiny is achieved by fasting. Thus Ramaḍān is a month of intensive training. Not only does it cultivate in us *Taqwā* and piety; it also trains us to acquire self-control. This leads to spiritual development as well as self-development.

We can only derive these benefits from fasting if we consciously set out to achieve these goals. If our fasting also becomes just another ritual, without soul and spirit, we will remain untouched by the blessings of this month. So as the Prophet (peace be upon him) reminds us, there are very many of us who do not achieve anything from fasting except hunger and thirst. Similarly many spend their time in night vigils but they only have sleepless nights (al-Dārimī). They fail to reap the spiritual insights and nearness to Allah (*swt*).

May Allah give us *Tawfīq* to perform our *'Ibādah* with sincerity and consciousness. May Allah accept our *Ṣiyām* (fasting) and *Qiyām* (night vigil) in this sacred month of Ramaḍān. (*Āmīn.*)

The Relationship Between Ramaḍān and the Qur'ān

يَٰٓأَيُّهَا ٱلنَّاسُ قَدْ جَآءَتْكُم مَّوْعِظَةٌ مِّن رَّبِّكُمْ وَشِفَآءٌ لِّمَا فِى ٱلصُّدُورِ وَهُدًى وَرَحْمَةٌ لِّلْمُؤْمِنِينَ ﴿٥٧﴾ قُلْ بِفَضْلِ ٱللَّهِ وَبِرَحْمَتِهِۦ فَبِذَٰلِكَ فَلْيَفْرَحُوا۟ هُوَ خَيْرٌ مِّمَّا يَجْمَعُونَ ﴿٥٨﴾

"O mankind! There has come to you an exhortation from your Lord, and a healing for what is in the breasts, and a guidance, and a mercy for believers." • Say: "In the bounty of Allah and His Mercy – in that let them rejoice; it is better than that they amass."

(Yūnus 10: 57–8)

Glory and greatness is for Allah (*swt*) and His Book. The Qur'ān is the greatest blessing bestowed on human beings. We are fortunate to be endowed with this blessing. This is the blessing of which there cannot be any comparison with any other blessing, as Allah, the Most Merciful has mentioned in the verses just recited. The four qualities of the Qur'ān enumerated in these verses are as follows:

First, the Qur'ān is an exhortation (*Maw'izah*) from Allah. People are living in ignorance. They are blindfolded and are being led towards their doom. They are oblivious of their predicament. Thus, the Glorious Qur'ān is an exhortation and an admonition to warn them of imminent danger. In other verses, Allah gives the additional qualities of the Qur'ān:

هَـٰذَا بَيَانٌ لِّلنَّاسِ وَهُدًى وَمَوْعِظَةٌ لِّلْمُتَّقِينَ ﴿١٣٨﴾

Here is a plain statement to people, a guidance and exhortation to those who fear Allah.

(Āl 'Imrān 3: 138)

يَـٰٓأَيُّهَا ٱلنَّاسُ قَدْ جَآءَكُم بُرْهَـٰنٌ مِّن رَّبِّكُمْ وَأَنزَلْنَآ إِلَيْكُمْ نُورًا مُّبِينًا ﴿١٧٤﴾

O mankind! Verily there has come to you a convincing proof from your Lord: for We have sent unto you a light (that is) manifest.

(al-Nisā' 4: 174)

Taking all these verses into account it is evident that the Glorious Qur'ān is a clear statement, a declaration with convincing proofs regarding basic beliefs. Thus, it should guide humanity towards the Right Path that is neither dark nor shrouded in mystery. It is the Straight Path that is manifest and brightly lit. It is in the interest of all human beings to pay heed to these exhortations and admonitions.

Second, the Qur'ān is a healing of hearts (*shifā' li mā fiṣ-ṣudūr*). The Qur'ān is a healing for diseases of the heart. According to Qur'ānic terminology the heart is not a pump which helps the circulation of blood, but rather it stands for the whole human personality – a person's emotions, motivations and his entire personality. This is well illustrated by many verses of the Qur'ān and *aḥādīth*:

فِى قُلُوبِهِم مَّرَضٌ ... ﴿١٠﴾

In their hearts is a disease.

(al-Baqarah 2: 10)

فَإِنَّهَا لَا تَعْمَى ٱلْأَبْصَـٰرُ وَلَـٰكِن تَعْمَى ٱلْقُلُوبُ ٱلَّتِى فِى ٱلصُّدُورِ ﴿٤٦﴾

Truly it is not their eyes that are blind, but their hearts which are in their breasts.

(al-Ḥajj 22: 46)

إِلَّا مَنْ أَتَى ٱللَّهَ بِقَلْبٍ سَلِيمٍ ﴿٨٩﴾

But only he (will prosper) that brings to Allah a sound heart.
(al-Shu'arā' 26: 89)

Narrated by 'Abdullāh al-Nu'mān ibn Bashīr

رَسُولَ اللَّهِ صَلَّى اللَّهُ عَلَيْهِ وَسَلَّمَ يَقُولُ أَلاَ وَإِنَّ فِي الْجَسَدِ مُضْغَةً
إِذَا صَلَحَتْ صَلَحَ الْجَسَدُ كُلُّهُ وَإِذَا فَسَدَتْ فَسَدَ الْجَسَدُ
كُلُّهُ أَلاَ وَهِيَ الْقَلْبُ

(متفق عليه)

Truly in the body there is a morsel of flesh which, if it be sound, the whole body is sound and which, if it be diseased, all of it is diseased. Truly it is the heart.
(Bukhārī and Muslim)

So what are diseases of the heart? Of course these are hypocrisy, envy, jealousy, pride, evil desires, corrupt motivations and the like. How does the Qur'ān cure these diseases? By inculcating *Taqwā* (God-Consciousness) and accountability on the Day of Judgement.

Third, the Qur'ān is a Book of Guidance. It enlightens human beings and provides them with inner insight that leads them to the Right Path:

وَٱلَّذِينَ ٱهْتَدَوْا۟ زَادَهُمْ هُدًى وَءَاتَىٰهُمْ تَقْوَىٰهُمْ ﴿١٧﴾

But to those who receive Guidance, He increases the (light of) Guidance, and bestows on them their Piety and Restraint (from evil).
(Muḥammad 47: 17)

Finally, one of the most manifest qualities of Allah (*swt*) is Mercy. His Mercy engulfs everything. The Revelation of the Holy Qur'ān is His act of Mercy:

ٱلرَّحۡمَٰنُ ۝١ عَلَّمَ ٱلۡقُرۡءَانَ ۝٢

(Allah) the Most Merciful! • It is He Who has taught the Qur'ān.

(al-Raḥmān 55: 1–2)

Thus, it is the Mercy of the Qur'ān that is saving humanity from the abyss of ignorance and leading them to light from darkness.

As there is no greater blessing than al-Qur'ān, Allah (*swt*) has decreed the month in which the Qur'ān was revealed as the Month of Blessing. The night in which the revelation began as the Night of Power (*Laylatul Qadr*) and the Night of Blessing (*Laylah Mubārakah*) and fasting is ordained in this month. Thus, when this Bounty and Mercy have come down it is incumbent upon mankind to be joyous and celebrate this event and honour His Guidance. In this way, the month of Ramaḍān is the celebration of the descent of Allah's Mercy and Guidance:

شَهۡرُ رَمَضَانَ ٱلَّذِيٓ أُنزِلَ فِيهِ ٱلۡقُرۡءَانُ هُدٗى لِّلنَّاسِ وَبَيِّنَٰتٖ مِّنَ
ٱلۡهُدَىٰ وَٱلۡفُرۡقَانِۚ فَمَن شَهِدَ مِنكُمُ ٱلشَّهۡرَ فَلۡيَصُمۡهُ ۝١٨٥

Ramaḍān is the month in which was sent down the Qur'ān, as a guide to mankind, also clear Signs for guidance and criterion (for judging right and wrong). So every one of you who is present during this month should fast.

(al-Baqarah 2: 185)

إِنَّآ أَنزَلۡنَٰهُ فِي لَيۡلَةِ ٱلۡقَدۡرِ ۝١

Indeed We have revealed this (al-Qur'ān) in the Night of Power.

(al-Qadr 97: 1)

إِنَّآ أَنزَلۡنَٰهُ فِي لَيۡلَةٖ مُّبَٰرَكَةٍۚ إِنَّا كُنَّا مُنذِرِينَ ۝٣

Indeed We sent it down during a Blessed Night for We wish to warn (against evil).

(al-Dukhān 44: 3)

Some may question the necessity of fasting in this blessed and joyous month. Let me explain. In order to receive the Guidance one needs preparation. As with a gardener, who wants to plant seeds, the soil has to be prepared before sowing. Similarly, hearts have to be prepared to receive this shower of Mercy. Only through this preparation will the soul germinate and prosper. This has been the practice of Allah throughout the ages. All Prophets have to spend time in fasting and seclusion before receiving Guidance from Allah. We know that our beloved Prophet (peace be upon him) spent many months in the Cave of Ḥirā' before receiving Revelations from Allah.

The other reason is that fasting creates *Taqwā* (God-Consciousness) which makes hearts receptive to Guidance. And just as we know that there are seasons and specific times for cultivating and planting shrubs and trees in the natural world, if we disregard them the trees will neither flourish nor bear fruit despite our utmost efforts. It is the same in the spiritual world. There are specific times and places, which are set aside, for cultivating souls and for concentrating on spiritual development. Thus, we observe *Jumuʿah* Prayers on a specific day and time. *Ḥajj* is performed in a specific month on prescribed dates. Similarly, the month of Ramaḍān is ordained for Fasting. The Night of *Qadr* is decreed to be better than a thousand months in its blessedness.

The Blessed month of Ramaḍān is with us. Are we preparing ourselves to receive this Guidance and Mercy from Allah (*swt*)? How should we rejoice in the Mercy and Blessing of Allah (*swt*)? How can we seek the treasures which await us in the Holy Qur'ān? Is this to be achieved by reading the Holy Qur'ān endlessly, turning pages laboriously, reciting its words beautifully, studying it in a most scholarly way? We do all these regularly but fail to collect its priceless gems and come away empty handed – souls untouched, hearts unmoved and our lives unchanged. The Blessings of the Qur'ān are limitless, but it depends on the capacity and suitability of our own receptacle which we bring to receive it.

We recite the Holy Qur'ān, sadly, often without any real understanding. For us, recitation (*tilāwah*) is mere reading without using the faculty of our hearts and minds. We have to enter the Qur'ān in the appropriate manner. What then is the appropriate manner? The Majestic Qur'ān explains it for us:

ٱلَّذِينَ ءَاتَيْنَٰهُمُ ٱلْكِتَٰبَ يَتْلُونَهُۥ حَقَّ تِلَاوَتِهِۦٓ أُو۟لَٰٓئِكَ يُؤْمِنُونَ بِهِۦ ۗ ... ﴿١٢١﴾

Those to whom We have given the Book, they recite it as it ought to be recited, it is they who believe in it.
(al-Baqarah 2: 121)

Tilāwah is to follow, not just to read: to abide closely with and go in pursuit of, to take it as a guide and to accept its authority. So, when we read, we should try to understand, follow, and act upon its Guidance. Thus, *tilāwah* involves our whole personality – soul, heart, mind, tongue and body. This is graphically illustrated by the Glorious Qur'ān:

إِنَّمَا ٱلْمُؤْمِنُونَ ٱلَّذِينَ إِذَا ذُكِرَ ٱللَّهُ وَجِلَتْ قُلُوبُهُمْ وَإِذَا تُلِيَتْ عَلَيْهِمْ
ءَايَٰتُهُۥ زَادَتْهُمْ إِيمَٰنًا وَعَلَىٰ رَبِّهِمْ يَتَوَكَّلُونَ ﴿٢﴾

For believers are those who, when Allah's name is mentioned, their hearts quake, and when His verses are recited to them their faith grows, and who put their trust in their Lord.
(al-Anfāl 8: 2)

ٱللَّهُ نَزَّلَ أَحْسَنَ ٱلْحَدِيثِ كِتَٰبًا مُّتَشَٰبِهًا مَّثَانِىَ تَقْشَعِرُّ مِنْهُ جُلُودُ ٱلَّذِينَ
يَخْشَوْنَ رَبَّهُمْ ثُمَّ تَلِينُ جُلُودُهُمْ وَقُلُوبُهُمْ إِلَىٰ ذِكْرِ ٱللَّهِ ۚ ... ﴿٢٣﴾

Allah has revealed the best discourse in the form of a Book, consistent with itself oft-repeating whereat shiver the skin of those who fear their Lord; then their skins and hearts soften to the remembrance of Allah.
(al-Zumar 39: 23)

The verse from *Sūrah Yūnus* quoted earlier is addressed to the whole of mankind, not just to Muslims. This clearly means that the Message needs to be transmitted to everyone, so that all human beings throughout all ages can benefit from it.

Two questions which emerge at this stage are: What efforts are we making to understand the message of the Holy Qur'ān? How are we preparing to extend the blessings of Allah (*swt*) to our fellow human beings?

These questions remind us of the true purpose of our lives. Come, let us join hands and engage ourselves in bringing the Message of the Holy Qur'ān to the people of this country. Let us remind the Muslim *Ummah* of its responsibility to present Islam to humanity at large. This is the means to gain the pleasure of Allah (*swt*) and the way to fulfil our purpose in life.

Let us pray that Allah, the Almighty may help us in disseminating the Message of the Holy Qur'ān. (*Āmīn.*)

Yawm al-Furqān: The Battle of Badr

إِن كُنتُمْ ءَامَنتُم بِٱللَّهِ وَمَآ أَنزَلْنَا عَلَىٰ عَبْدِنَا يَوْمَ ٱلْفُرْقَانِ يَوْمَ
ٱلْتَقَى ٱلْجَمْعَانِ ۗ وَٱللَّهُ عَلَىٰ كُلِّ شَىْءٍ قَدِيرٌ ﴿٤١﴾ إِذْ أَنتُم
بِٱلْعُدْوَةِ ٱلدُّنْيَا وَهُم بِٱلْعُدْوَةِ ٱلْقُصْوَىٰ وَٱلرَّكْبُ أَسْفَلَ
مِنكُمْ ۚ وَلَوْ تَوَاعَدتُّمْ لَٱخْتَلَفْتُمْ فِى ٱلْمِيعَٰدِ ۙ وَلَٰكِن لِّيَقْضِىَ
ٱللَّهُ أَمْرًا كَانَ مَفْعُولًا لِّيَهْلِكَ مَنْ هَلَكَ عَنۢ بَيِّنَةٍ وَيَحْيَىٰ
مَنْ حَىَّ عَنۢ بَيِّنَةٍ ۗ وَإِنَّ ٱللَّهَ لَسَمِيعٌ عَلِيمٌ ﴿٤٢﴾

If you do believe in Allah and in the Revelation We sent down to Our Servant on the Day of Testing – the Day of the meeting of the two forces. For Allah has power over all things. Remember you were on the near side of the valley, and they on the farther side, and the caravan on the lower ground than you. Even if you had made a mutual appointment to meet, you would certainly have failed in the appointment: But (thus you met) so that Allah might accomplish a matter already enacted: that those who died might die after a clear sign (had been given). And those who lived might live after a clear sign (had been given). And verily Allah is He who hears and knows (all things).

(al-Anfāl 8: 41–2)

This is how Allah (*swt*) describes the Battle of Badr in *Sūrah al-Anfāl.* The Battle of Badr is a beacon of light that still shines through the pages of Islamic history. Even after the passage of over fourteen hundred years, it provides guidance to the *Ummah* on how to achieve glorious victory against all the odds. It gives hope and courage that people with scarce resources and meagre manpower can defeat a mighty well-armed force with the help of their *Īmān* and morale and of course with the help of Allah (*swt*).

Historians agree that the Battle of Badr was fought on Friday, 17 Ramaḍān in the second year of Ḥijrah. The battleground lay 92 miles west of Madinah and about 160 miles north of Makkah. The reason behind this encounter was the bitter opposition and disappointment that the Quraysh felt at the establishment of a successful Islamic State in Madinah. They sought to crush it somehow. This opportunity arose when Abū Sufyān was accompanying a large trade caravan from Syria. As the route of the caravan passed close to Madinah he was fearful that the Muslims would attack it. He called for help by sending an emissary to Makkah. The Quraysh quickly raised an army of over a thousand men and horses, together with camels, arms and ammunitions to mount an attack.

The Prophet (peace be upon him) assembled all the Muslims and explained the situation. Abū Bakr al-Ṣiddīq (may Allah be pleased with him) led the *Muhājirīn* and 'Umar ibn al-Khaṭṭāb (may Allah be pleased with him) endorsed the decision to prepare for battle. On behalf of the *Muhājirīn,* al-Miqdād (may Allah be pleased with him) said: "O Prophet of Allah! Wherever your Lord wants you to go you proceed there and we will follow you. We are not like Banī Isrā'īl who told Mūsā (peace be upon him), 'you and your Lord should go and fight while we will sit here'. What we say is you and your Lord fight and we will fight with you."

Then the Prophet (peace be upon him) turned towards the *Anṣār.* Sa'd ibn 'Ubādah (may Allah be pleased with him) got up and said: "O Prophet of Allah! We believed in your Prophethood. We proclaim your Truthfulness. Please go wherever you like and we will accompany you. By God, if you ask us to cross the ocean and you jump and we will follow you."

This shows the unity and love for sacrifice of the Companions. Thus, 313 joined the army of the Prophet and marched towards Badr. By this time, Abū Sufyān was able to bypass Madinah taking an easterly route near the Red Sea. He urged the Makkans to withdraw, as there was no danger to the caravan. Yet Abū Jahl insisted that the Makkan army should take the Muslims on and crush them.

The plain which the Prophet (peace be upon him) chose was sandy high ground and the Muslim army had access to water. By the grace of Allah (*swt*) it rained during the night. It made the sand firm whereas the Makkans who were on lower ground found themselves stuck in the mire. The battle started and there was fierce fighting. This was the first time in Arab history that people of the same tribes fought against each other not for tribal rivalries but for the sake of their Faiths. The Prophet was in Prayer seeking Allah's help. Prostrating, he said: "O Allah, if these few people were to be defeated no one will ever worship You." Then he came out and urged everyone to fight with their utmost strength. He said: "By God, whoever fights with patience and perseverance in the way of Allah and who keeps moving forward and does not turn back he will certainly enter Paradise." The brother of ʿUmar ibn al-Hammām banī Salamah was eating dates and he heard this from the Prophet and said: "Very well, O Prophet. Really, is the distance between *Jannah* and me only that they kill me?" He threw down his dates and picked up a sword and dived onto the battlefield and fought bravely until he was martyred. And there were many other such acts of courage.

Allah did help the Muslims with an invisible force of angels. The Makkans were defeated and many notable leaders including Abū Jahl were killed. Conversely, the Muslims suffered few losses. Many Makkans, however, were made prisoners of war, and these were distributed among the Companions. The Prophet (peace be upon him) instructed that they should be treated humanely.

Abū ʿUzair, who was the flag-bearer of the Makkans, was arrested by an *Anṣārī* and Muṣʿab ibn ʿUmair who was his real brother saw this and asked that the *Anṣārī* tie him firmly as his mother was a wealthy lady and would pay a huge ransom. Abū ʿUzair retorted to the effect that Muṣʿab you are my brother and you are saying this. Muṣʿab replied:

"This *Anṣārī* is my brother prior to you." Eventually his mother sent four thousand *dīnars* by way of ransom. Additionally the Muslims also acquired a large booty from this battle.

This is, in brief, the factual description of this famous Battle. What lessons have we to learn from this today? First, it is the *Sunnah* of Allah (*swt*) to test those who say they believe. So trials and other hardships are inflicted to test our sincerity. This is part of our training, it makes us firm in our resolve and commitment. Second, only those who stand firm and face all hardships and who are willing to sacrifice their lives will eventually receive Allah's help. Just praying for Allah's help without making any effort will not lead us to success. Third, when we are asked to make sacrifices in the way of Allah we hesitate as we have other priorities and we keep on eating our "dates". Those who do this will never succeed. Finally, we should realise that the relationship of Faith is stronger than that of blood ties and if there is some conflict between our duty to our Faith and to our kith and kin then as a believer we should be clear in our mind where our duty lies.

Let us pray that Allah may keep us steadfast in our *Īmān* and that we prepare ourselves for the supreme sacrifice in the way of Allah. Let not the glitter and attraction of this worldly life detract us from the path of Jihād. (*Āmīn.*)

Laylatul Qadr

إِنَّآ أَنزَلْنَٰهُ فِى لَيْلَةِ ٱلْقَدْرِ ﴿١﴾ وَمَآ أَدْرَىٰكَ مَا لَيْلَةُ ٱلْقَدْرِ ﴿٢﴾ لَيْلَةُ
ٱلْقَدْرِ خَيْرٌ مِّنْ أَلْفِ شَهْرٍ ﴿٣﴾ تَنَزَّلُ ٱلْمَلَٰٓئِكَةُ وَٱلرُّوحُ فِيهَا بِإِذْنِ
رَبِّهِم مِّن كُلِّ أَمْرٍ ﴿٤﴾ سَلَٰمٌ هِىَ حَتَّىٰ مَطْلَعِ ٱلْفَجْرِ ﴿٥﴾

We have indeed revealed this (Message) in the Night of Power • And what will explain to you what the Night of Power is? • The Night of Power is better than a thousand months • Therein come down the Angels and the Spirit by Allah's permission, on every errand • Peace! There is until the rise of morning.

(al-Qadr 97: 1–5)

The entirety of *Sūrah al-Qadr* which is just recited highlights the importance of the Qur'ān and its *Barakah*. Allah (*swt*) has designated the night in which revelation of the Holy Qur'ān began as the Night of Power. In *Sūrah al-Dukhān* it is called *Lailah Mubārakah* (the Blessed Night):

حمٓ ﴿١﴾ وَٱلْكِتَٰبِ ٱلْمُبِينِ ﴿٢﴾ إِنَّآ أَنزَلْنَٰهُ فِى لَيْلَةٍ مُّبَٰرَكَةٍ ... ﴿٣﴾

Ḥā Mīm • *By the Book that makes things clear • We sent it down during a Blessed Night...*

(al-Dukhān 44: 1–3)

As we know the Revelation started in the month of Ramaḍān. Thus, *Laylatul Qadr* is one of the nights in Ramaḍān. What does *Qadr* mean?

Qadr means to have power or choice. One of the attributes of Allah (*swt*) is *Qadīr* (One who has power over everything). It is narrated in certain *aḥādīth* that Allah (*swt*) ordained everything in this universe and His decisions about the whole year are made and conveyed to angels during this Night:

تَنَزَّلُ ٱلْمَلَٰٓئِكَةُ وَٱلرُّوحُ فِيهَا بِإِذْنِ رَبِّهِم مِّن كُلِّ أَمْرٍ ﴿٤﴾

Therein come down the Angels and the Spirit by Allah's permission, on every errand.

(al-Qadr 97: 4)

Human beings reckon time as past, present and future, but for Allah (*swt*) everything is in His knowledge so there is no such period as the future. But to implement His plan for the Universe and for the angels to carry out His Plan, it is on this Night that it is passed on to them. Thus, during this Night important affairs are determined. This is mentioned in *Sūrah al-Dukhān*:

فِيهَا يُفْرَقُ كُلُّ أَمْرٍ حَكِيمٍ ﴿٤﴾

In this (Night) is made distinct every affair of wisdom.

(al-Dukhān 44: 4)

Qadr also means value and importance. This meaning conveys the importance and value of the Qur'ān that it was revealed during this Night for the Guidance of mankind. Some *'Ulamā'* say that on this night the whole of the Qur'ān from *Lawḥ Maḥfūz* – the well-protected Tablet – was passed on to the angels. Then for the next 23 years it was revealed piecemeal. Others are of the opinion that it means that this is the Night of the First Revelation.

And how would you know what Laylatul Qadr *is?* This rhetorical question signifies the value, esteem and importance of this Night. The question is posed to increase the motivation to understand its value and importance. The statement that it is *Better than a thousand months* according to Imām al-Rāzī indicates immeasurable quantity. It does not mean just one thousand months but hundreds and thousands of months and years. It is customary in the Arabic language to use the number of a thousand to indicate immeasurable quantity.

How is it better than a thousand months? Allah has used the word *Khair* meaning goodness. Thus *'Ibādah* in this Night is equal to *'Ibādah* to the value of a thousand months. There is also a *ḥadīth* narrated by Abū Hurairah that says:

مَنْ قَامَ لَيْلَةَ الْقَدْرِ إِيمَانًا وَاحْتِسَابًا غُفِرَ لَهُ مَا تَقَدَّمَ مِنْ ذَنْبِه

(متفق عليه)

Those who stand up in prayers in *Laylatul Qadr* with *Īmān* and *Iḥtisāb* their previous sins are forgiven.
(Bukhārī and Muslim)

This *Qiyām* in *Laylatul Qadr* should be in the state of *Īmān* and with *Iḥtisāb*. *Īmān* and *Iḥtisāb* are technical words in Islamic terminology. They mean that all good actions are done for the sake of Allah (*swt*) with the hope of receiving reward from Him. Thus, there should not be any other motive. *Iḥtisāb* means scrutiny. We should take account of all our sins and shortcomings and seek Allah's forgiveness. If we are sincere in our repentance and Prayers Allah, the Most Merciful, the Most Kind will forgive us, *Inshā' Allāh*.

Thus *'Ibādah* in the form of *Ṣalāh*, *Istighfār*, *Tilāwah* and seeking forgiveness and *Du'ā'* in this Blessed Night are rewarded a thousand fold. One of the reasons for this generous reward is that believers of the earlier *Ummah* enjoyed long lives as compared to today's Muslim *Ummah*, and thus they were able to accumulate more rewards. Allah gave this *Ummah* a precious Night so that we can accumulate greater rewards as well. However, the real reason for the blessedness, value and esteem of this Night is due to the Revelation of the Qur'ān commencing on this Night. This is the Book that has changed the course of history for over a thousand years. What was Revealed in this Night will shape the destiny of humanity forever.

Which night of Ramaḍān is *Laylatul Qadr*? *Mufassirūn* differ in pinpointing the specific Night of *Qadr*. In *Ṣaḥīḥ aḥādīth*, the Prophet (peace be upon him) instructed us to locate it in the last ten nights of Ramaḍān and it is further indicated that it is one of the odd nights that is the 21st, 23rd, 25th, 27th or 29th of Ramaḍān. From these five nights, most *'Ulamā'* believe it is the 27th night. Thus the majority of Muslims celebrate *Laylatul Qadr* on the 27th night. In most mosques, the ceremony of *Khatmul Qur'ān* (completion of the recitation of the whole Qur'ān) is held on the 27th night of Ramaḍān. Most Muslims observe *Qiyām al-Layl* (night vigil) on this night. However, the reason for not pinpointing the exact Night is that in order to receive the blessing of *Laylatul Qadr* people should spend most nights of the last ten days of Ramaḍān in *'Ibādah* and not restrict themselves to one night only.

What should we ask Allah (*swt*) on this Blessed Night? This was the question *Umm al-Mu'minīn* 'Ā'ishah (may Allah be pleased with her) inquired from the Prophet (peace be upon him). He taught her this Prayer:

اللَّهُمَّ إِنَّكَ عَفُوٌّ تُحِبُّ الْعَفْوَ فَاعْفُ عَنِّي

(احمد والترمذي وابن ماجة)

O Allah! You are most forgiving and You love forgiving,
(please) do forgive (my sins).
(Aḥmad, Tirmidhī, Ibn Mājah)

Thus, in these last few days of Ramaḍān we should concentrate on *'Ibādah* and seek forgiveness from Allah (*swt*) and pray that Allah (*swt*) save us from the damnation of the Fire. May Allah (*swt*) give us *Tawfīq* to receive the full blessings of *Laylatul Qadr*. (*Āmīn.*)

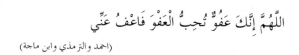

ʿĪd al-Fiṭr

وَلِتُكۡمِلُواْ ٱلۡعِدَّةَ وَلِتُكَبِّرُواْ ٱللَّهَ عَلَىٰ مَا هَدَىٰكُمۡ
وَلَعَلَّكُمۡ تَشۡكُرُونَ ١٨٥

And He desires that you complete the prescribed period [of fasting]. And glorify God for His Guidance to you; that you may be grateful.

(al-Baqarah 2: 185)

Every nation and every state celebrate festivals of their own. These celebrations create homogeneity and a collective consciousness that sustains the unity and cohesiveness of a nation. When the Prophet (peace be upon him) migrated to Madinah he found that the people of Madinah – a large majority of them now Muslim – celebrated two festivals and used to play games, compete in sports and have other entertainments. The Prophet (peace be upon him) asked them about the significance of these two days. They replied that they celebrated them during the period of *Jāhilīyah* – the period of Ignorance before Islam – and hence they continued with this tradition. The Prophet (peace be upon him) said: "Allah has given two better festivals for you [and they are] the day of *ʿĪd al-Aḍḥā* and the day of *ʿĪd al-Fiṭr*" (Abū Dā'ūd).

As festivals reflect the beliefs and history of a people, the Prophet (peace be upon him) changed the customs of the period of Ignorance with the Islamic Faith's identity. In this respect, he prescribed two festivals that signify Islamic belief and culture.

Usually the festivals that nations and religions celebrate commemorate important events or landmarks in their history or the birth or death of their founders who created their distinct identity. Our festival of *'Īd* does not celebrate even the birth of the Prophet Muḥammad (peace be upon him), though he was the founder of the Muslim *Ummah*, he was the last Messenger who brought the Divine Guidance to mankind and a great mercy from God unto the world. Rather, it celebrates the sending down of the Word of God, the Qur'ān, and its triumph.

Thus, instead of rejoicing at the beginning of a new year, celebrating the ending of the dark days of winter, the dawn of spring, midsummer day, or thanksgiving for harvest, *'Īd al-Fiṭr* is the offering of thanks for completing the soul's purification represented by fasting in the blessed month of Ramaḍān. It is also an occasion of thanksgiving for receiving the richest blessings of Allah – the blessed Qur'ān – for enriching our souls and minds, for guiding human beings to live in peace and harmony in this world and achieve success in the Hereafter. This rejoicing is ordained by Allah (*swt*) in *Sūrah Yūnus*:

يَٰٓأَيُّهَا ٱلنَّاسُ قَدْ جَآءَتْكُم مَّوْعِظَةٌ مِّن رَّبِّكُمْ وَشِفَآءٌ لِّمَا فِى
ٱلصُّدُورِ وَهُدًى وَرَحْمَةٌ لِّلْمُؤْمِنِينَ ﴿٥٧﴾ قُلْ بِفَضْلِ ٱللَّهِ وَبِرَحْمَتِهِۦ
فَبِذَٰلِكَ فَلْيَفْرَحُوا۟ هُوَ خَيْرٌ مِّمَّا يَجْمَعُونَ ﴿٥٨﴾

O mankind! Now there has come unto you an admonition from your Lord, and a healing for the (diseases) in your hearts and a Guidance and a Mercy for those who believe • Say: "In the Bounty of Allah and in His Mercy – in that let them rejoice; for it is better than all that they may amass."
(Yūnus 10: 57–8)

'Īd is not just a spiritual and solemn occasion, it is a great day for rejoicing and merriment all over the world for Muslims. New clothes, the decoration of houses, mosques, the preparation of delicious dishes, and the exchange of greeting cards and gifts creates a feeling of joy and delight. Yet those who are poor and needy are not forgotten in this festival. It is made compulsory for everyone to pay *Ṣadaqah al-Fiṭr* – a charity so that the poverty-stricken can also participate in this joyous occasion.

So on *'Īd* Day Muslims are recommended to have a bath, put on their best dress and perfume and assemble for Congregational Prayers, which are performed after sunrise. It is recommended that *ʿĪd* Prayers be held in open spaces so that large numbers of Muslims from one part of the city can assemble there. Women and children are also encouraged to attend. This shows the solidarity of the Muslim *Ummah*. They should walk or drive to Mosques and Prayer Halls, chanting:

Allah is the Greatest! Allah is the Greatest!	اللهُ أَكْبَرُ اللهُ أَكْبَر
There is no deity save Allah!	لاَ إِلَهَ إِلاَّ اللهُ
Allah is the Greatest! Allah is the Greatest!	اللهُ أَكْبَرُ اللهُ أَكْبَر
And all thankful praise is to Allah!	وَلِلَّهِ الْحَمْد

It is narrated in a *ḥadīth* that angels stand on both sides of the roads on *ʿĪd* Day and proclaim:

أُغْدُوا يَامَعْشَرَ الْمُسْلِمِينَ إِلَى رَبٍّ كَرِيمٍ يَمُنُّ بِالْخَيْرِ ثُمَّ يُثِيبُ عَلَيْهِ الثَّوَابَ الْجَزِيلَ لَقَدْ أُمِرْتُمْ بِقِيَامِ اللَّيْلِ فَقُمْتُمْ، وَأُمِرْتُمْ بِصِيَامِ النَّهَارِ فَصُمْتُمْ، وَأَطَعْتُمْ رَبَّكُمْ فَأَقْبِضُوا جَوَائِزَكُمْ

(الطبراني)

"O Believers! Walk towards your Lord Who is the most Generous. He favours you with goodness and virtue and gives you great reward. He commanded you to pray during the night and fast during the day. Now that you have obeyed Him, come and receive your rewards."

And as the believers finish their *ʿĪd* Prayer they again say:

أَلاَ إِنَّ رَبَّكُمْ قَدْ غَفَرَ لَكُمْ فَارْجِعُوا رَاشِدِينَ إِلَى رِحَالِكُمْ فَهُوَ يَوْمُ الْجَائِزَةِ، وَيُسَمَّى ذَالِكَ الْيَوْمُ فِي السَّمَاءِ يَوْمُ الْجَائِزَةِ

(الطبراني)

"Allah has forgiven you. Return to your homes with the best of good and glad tidings. This is the day of reward. This day is called the day of reward in heaven as well."

(Ṭabarānī)

It is the day when Muslims visit friends and relatives and exchange greetings by embracing each other and saying *'Īd Mubārak*. This expression of brotherly love with a purity of heart is the best gift of *'Īd*.

In Islam, all *'Ibādah* and activities are performed communally. So *'Īd* is no different. Thus on *'Īd* Day family and community are the focus of festivity. This can only happen if *'Īd* is to be celebrated on the same day by Muslims living in the same city. It is a tragedy that our *'Ulamā'* cannot reach any consensus on the sighting of the new moon for the beginning of Ramaḍān and for *'Īd*. Islam is a natural religion, based on reason. The times of the five daily Prayers are regulated by the movements of the sun. The sighting of the new moon regulates the beginning and end of a month. These phenomena are observable all over the world. In this country, we are not able to observe the sun every day and, thus, we rely on the observatory to give us precise information about sunrise, sunset and the time when the sun will be at its zenith. Tremendous advancements in astronomy can give us accurate information on the visibility of the new moon in any locality. This could be one way of arriving at such a consensus. Another alternative is to accept the sighting of the moon in any Muslim country which is acceptable to all *'Ulamā'*. Or another way should be found to resolve this confusion which is faced every year by Muslims living in non-Muslim countries. Otherwise, not only do we fail to reap the blessings of *'Īd* but we are the target of ridicule by non-Muslims. It also creates problems for schools and factories and offices where half of the Muslims take time off one day and others on the next. If there is unity among us, we can persuade the Government and educational institutions to give an optional holiday to Muslim workers and students on that day. Either way, this chaos should end.

Let us celebrate *'Īd* to express our intense gratitude and praise to Allah. Let us commit ourselves to the striving and the struggle to bring God's choicest gifts in the Blessed Qur'ān to ourselves and to all humanity. May Allah help us in our resolve. (*Āmīn.*)

Ḥajj: A Season of Reawakening

وَأَذِّن فِي ٱلنَّاسِ بِٱلْحَجِّ يَأْتُوكَ رِجَالًا وَعَلَىٰ كُلِّ ضَامِرٍ يَأْتِينَ مِن
كُلِّ فَجٍّ عَمِيقٍ ﴿٢٧﴾ لِّيَشْهَدُوا۟ مَنَٰفِعَ لَهُمْ وَيَذْكُرُوا۟ ٱسْمَ ٱللَّهِ فِيٓ أَيَّامٍ
مَّعْلُومَٰتٍ عَلَىٰ مَا رَزَقَهُم مِّنۢ بَهِيمَةِ ٱلْأَنْعَٰمِ ۖ فَكُلُوا۟ مِنْهَا وَأَطْعِمُوا۟
ٱلْبَآئِسَ ٱلْفَقِيرَ ﴿٢٨﴾ ثُمَّ لْيَقْضُوا۟ تَفَثَهُمْ وَلْيُوفُوا۟ نُذُورَهُمْ
وَلْيَطَّوَّفُوا۟ بِٱلْبَيْتِ ٱلْعَتِيقِ ﴿٢٩﴾

And proclaim the Pilgrimage among people: they will come to you on foot and (mounted) on every kind of camel, lean on account of journeys through deep and distant mountain highways • that they may witness the benefits (provided) for them, and celebrate the name of Allah, through the days appointed, over cattle which He has provided for them (for sacrifice): then eat you thereof and feed the distressed ones in want • Let them complete the rites prescribed for them, perform their vows, and (again) circumambulate the Ancient House.

(al-Ḥajj 22: 27–9).

In accordance with the command of Allah (*swt*) the call for *Ḥajj* first given by the Prophet Ibrāhīm (peace be upon him) is proclaimed every year and has been for the last four thousand years. Muslims from all over the world, using different modes of transport, assemble on the Plain of ʿArafāt responding:

لَبَّيْكَ اللَّهُمَّ لَبَّيْكَ لَبَّيْكَ لاَ شَرِيكَ لَكَ لَبَّيْكَ إِنَّ الْحَمْدَ وَالنِّعْمَةَ لَكَ
وَالْمُلْكَ لاَ شَرِيكَ لَكَ

Here I am O Allah, here I am. Here I am. You have no partners, here I am. Verily all praise and dominion is Yours, and You have no partner.

Allah (*swt*) has made us one *Ummah* so that we remain united in His worship and obedience and thus receive His blessings and mercy. In *Sūrah al-Anbiyā'* Allah says:

إِنَّ هَٰذِهِۦٓ أُمَّتُكُمْ أُمَّةً وَٰحِدَةً وَأَنَا۠ رَبُّكُمْ فَٱعْبُدُونِ ﴿٩٢﴾

Verily, this Ummah *of yours is a single* Ummah *and I am your Lord and Cherisher: therefore serve Me (and no other).*
(al-Anbiyā' 21: 92)

The *Kalimah* (the Declaration of Faith) which we recite to proclaim our *Īmān* and *Tawḥīd* of Allah (*swt*) also establishes the bonds of brotherhood among us. Thus, all our *'Ibādah* (acts of worship) promotes and manifests this *Ukhuwwah* (brotherhood). It is recommended that we pray in *Jamā'ah* (congregation). We fast together in the month of Ramaḍān. Above all, it is during the *Ḥajj* season when pilgrims from all over the world, assemble at the same place and at the same time donning un-sewn pieces of cloth, that the homogeneity and unity of the *Ummah* is manifested for all to see. This eliminates all distinctions of nationality, colour or language. All differences are discarded and all unite in worship of Allah. Even the rest of the *Ummah* joins those who are performing *Ḥajj* by reciting special *Tasbīḥ* after *Farḍ* Prayers from the 9th to the 13th of Dhū al-Ḥijjah. Muslims all over the world celebrate *'Īd al-Aḍḥā* and sacrifice animals, thus, associating themselves *in absentia* with pilgrims. This unifying aspect of *Ḥajj* has impressed the rest of the world. Robert Bianchi in his article on *Ḥajj* in the *Oxford Encylopaedia of the Modern Islamic World* (Vol. 2, p. 88) observes:

> Unique among the world's great pilgrimages, the *ḥajj* is in many ways also the most important. Even compared to the ancient

> and highly developed international pilgrimage systems of Christianity and Hinduism, the *ḥajj* is remarkable in its doctrinal centrality, its geographic focus, and its historical continuity. The size and global coverage of the *ḥajj* are unparalleled. It regularly attracts one million overseas pilgrims from virtually every nation. The combined contingents form the largest and most culturally diverse assembly of humanity in one place at one time.

Like all other Islamic teachings the rituals performed during *Ḥajj* were prescribed to cement our relations and create solidarity. Prof. Khurshid Ahmad explains this aspect of *Ḥajj* as follows:

> One other unique aspect of *Ḥajj* is that it manifests the unity of the *Ummah* and all of humankind as one family and tribe. It eliminates all differences of colour, race, language, nationality, social status, and economic disparity. All believers in Allah gather together from every corner of the earth for pilgrimage and *ṭawāf* of the House of Allah. They live together like one family and under the leadership of an Imām recite *Talbiyah*. All outward coverings of culture and civilization lay bare and only Godliness and humanity are presented as a model.
>
> (*Tarjumān al-Qur'ān*, April 1998, p. 10)

Why are we not able to reap the benefits of *Ḥajj*, which is performed by two million Muslims every year? We should seriously reflect on the reasons behind our shortcomings. These are not, however, far to seek. We perform the rites and rituals of *Ḥajj* but the real soul has vanished. Many people go on *Ḥajj* when they are in the last stages of their lives. Many who go are illiterate and unaware of the revolutionary aspects of Islamic teachings, whereas the acquisition of knowledge is the prime duty of every Muslim, male or female. Thus, *Ḥajj* is performed without a conscious effort to understand its purpose and to assimilate its true spirit. When all our *'Ibādah* become routine rituals and habits bereft of its soul there is no doubt that we do not receive their full blessings and beneficial results.

A person came to see Junaid al-Baghdādī (may Allah have mercy on him) after performing *Ḥajj*. The following conversation is recorded by

Shaikh ʿUthmān ibn ʿAlī al-Hujwīrī (may Allah have mercy on him) in his famous book *Kashf al-Maḥjūb*: "When you said goodbye and left your home for *Ḥajj*, did you say goodbye to your sinful life as well?" He said: "No". "During the journey when you traversed from one place to the other, did you traverse towards nearness to Allah as well?" He replied: "No". "When you discarded your worldly clothes and put on *Iḥrām*, did you discard your imperfections from your life?" He answered: "No". "When you did *Ṭawāf* of the Kaʿbah, did you see the gracious beauty of Allah?" He said: "No". "When you did *saʿī* of Ṣafā and Marwah, did you attain *Ṣafā* (Purity) and *Muruwwah* (goodness)?" He replied: "No". "When you went to Minā, did your worldly *Minā* (Ambitions) also cease?" He replied: "No". "When you stayed in ʿArafāt, did you spend any time in *ʿIrfān* (Knowing) of Allah?" He said: "No". "When you were slaughtering did you slaughter your carnal self as well?" He said: "No". Then Junaid al-Baghdādī (may Allah be pleased with him) advised him, "You really did not make your journey to *Ḥajj*, as you did not experience and achieve the things I have mentioned. Go back and do as I told you, only then will you reach *Maqām Ibrāhīm*."

Thus, it is essential that we try and recreate the consciousness through education and *daʿwah* among the masses so that they understand the real Message of Islam and mould their lives according to Islamic teachings. It is only through such efforts that the *Ummah* can retain its identity and attain unity. As Sayyid Abul Aʿlā Mawdūdī (may Allah have mercy on him) has observed:

> *Ḥajj* [is a season] of reawakening and a rebirth of hearts and societies. The Wise One who has given us the *Sharīʿah* has thus ensured that whatever adverse turn world conditions may take and however bad the times may become, they will never succeed in erasing the universal Islamic movement so long as the Kaʿbah is there.
>
> For, it has been placed in the body of the Islamic world just like a heart in the man's body. As long as the heart beats, a man cannot die. In exactly the same way this "heart of the world" draws blood from its far-off veins and circulates the blood back into each and every artery. As long as this throbbing of the heart

> continues and as long as this process of drawing the blood and circulating it lasts, it will be impossible to end the life of this body of the Muslim *Ummah*, however run-down disease may have made it.
>
> (*Let us be Muslims*, pp. 274–5)

It is our misfortune that we neglect to take benefit from this world assembly of Muslims. We can still revitalise and rejuvenate the *Ummah* if we sincerely try to understand the significance of *Ḥajj* and perform it with true spirit.

We earnestly pray that Allah (*swt*) may guide us and we as individuals and as a *Jamāʿah* undertake the mission of fulfilling the duties of this *Ummah* and attain success in this world and salvation in the Hereafter. (*Āmīn.*)

Sacrifice

قُلْ إِنَّ صَلَاتِي وَنُسُكِي وَمَحْيَايَ وَمَمَاتِي لِلَّهِ رَبِّ ٱلْعَالَمِينَ ﴿١٦٢﴾

Say: "Truly my prayer and my service of sacrifice, my life and my death are (all) for Allah, the Cherisher of the Worlds."
(al-An'ām 6: 162)

If someone were to ask you what is Islam how would you answer? You may start by enumerating upon the Five Pillars or explaining the meaning of the word "Islam" and the requirement to submit to the will of Allah. There are pamphlets and books elucidating all aspects of Islamic beliefs and teachings. These may help someone to understand but may still leave many aspects unanswered. This is very similar to a lay person asking about the workings of complicated machinery, such as aircraft engines or electron microscopes. Any amount of verbal explanation and written material may still leave him bewildered. It is much easier, therefore to give a better explanation if you have a model at hand. The person inquiring can then see for himself and can follow the explanations given of how things work.

To see the model of Islam is to see the life of the Prophet Ibrāhīm (peace be upon him). The salient features of his personality are manifested in his life of total submission to and obedience of Allah (*swt*).

To start with, the direction of his life was entirely focused towards Allah. He said:

إِنِّي وَجَّهْتُ وَجْهِيَ لِلَّذِي فَطَرَ ٱلسَّمَٰوَٰتِ وَٱلْأَرْضَ
حَنِيفًا ۖ وَمَآ أَنَا۠ مِنَ ٱلْمُشْرِكِينَ ﴿٧٩﴾

For me, I have set my face, firmly and truly, towards Him who created the heavens and the earth, and never shall I make partners to Allah.

(al-An'ām 6: 79)

To implement this conviction we see that all his relations and dealings with his family, his society and his nation, whether personal or societal, were governed strictly under Divine supremacy. He firmly enjoined himself to Allah and severed all other relationships. He left his home, his parents and his birthplace to wander in the wilderness rather than compromise his beliefs. So complete and thorough was his submission that no sooner was he asked to submit then he instantaneously submitted himself to the Divine will:

إِذْ قَالَ لَهُۥ رَبُّهُۥٓ أَسْلِمْ ۖ قَالَ أَسْلَمْتُ لِرَبِّ ٱلْعَٰلَمِينَ ﴿١٣١﴾

Behold! His Lord said to him "Bow (your will to Me)": He said: "I bow (my will) to the Lord and Cherisher of the Universe."

(al-Baqarah 2: 131)

He was extremely selfless and sincere for the cause of the propagation of the Divine Message. Thus, he was not worried about his own well-being, but was concerned that the Message of Allah be perpetuated not only in his lifetime but in the centuries to come. He established institutions and society in such a way that future generations should continue to be blessed. For this purpose, he and his son Ismā'īl built the Ka'bah, the first House on earth for the worship of Allah. Then, he established the institution of *Ḥajj* and his earnest prayer for the Muslim *Ummah* to continue his mission. These efforts are the testimony of his love, devotion and far-sightedness so that the Oneness of Allah (*swt*) continues to permeate throughout the ages. Thus, when he was laying the foundation of the Ka'bah with his son Ismā'īl, they prayed:

رَبَّنَا وَٱجۡعَلۡنَا مُسۡلِمَيۡنِ لَكَ وَمِن ذُرِّيَّتِنَآ أُمَّةٗ مُّسۡلِمَةٗ لَّكَ وَأَرِنَا
مَنَاسِكَنَا وَتُبۡ عَلَيۡنَآۖ إِنَّكَ أَنتَ ٱلتَّوَّابُ ٱلرَّحِيمُ ﴿١٢٨﴾ رَبَّنَا وَٱبۡعَثۡ
فِيهِمۡ رَسُولٗا مِّنۡهُمۡ يَتۡلُواْ عَلَيۡهِمۡ ءَايَٰتِكَ وَيُعَلِّمُهُمُ ٱلۡكِتَٰبَ
وَٱلۡحِكۡمَةَ وَيُزَكِّيهِمۡۚ إِنَّكَ أَنتَ ٱلۡعَزِيزُ ٱلۡحَكِيمُ ﴿١٢٩﴾

Our Lord! Make us Muslims, bowing to Your (will) and our progeny a community Muslim, bowing to your (Will)... • Our Lord! Send amongst them a Messenger of their own, who shall rehearse Your Signs to them and instruct them in Scripture and Wisdom, and sanctify them: for You are the Exalted in Might, the Wise.

(al-Baqarah 2: 128–9)

Above all, his life was full of sacrifices. The supreme test came when he was asked by Allah (*swt*) to sacrifice his son. Without hesitation both father and son submitted themselves in obedience:

فَلَمَّآ أَسۡلَمَا وَتَلَّهُۥ لِلۡجَبِينِ ﴿١٠٣﴾ وَنَٰدَيۡنَٰهُ أَن يَٰٓإِبۡرَٰهِيمُ ﴿١٠٤﴾
قَدۡ صَدَّقۡتَ ٱلرُّءۡيَآۚ ... ﴿١٠٥﴾

So when they both submitted their wills (to Allah), and he had laid him prostrate on his forehead (for sacrifice) • We called out to him "O Ibrāhīm! • You have already fulfilled the vision."

(al-Ṣāffāt 37: 103–5)

Yet another perfect model we find in the life of the Prophet Muḥammad (peace be upon him). He was persecuted in Makkah, stoned and ridiculed in Taif, and suffered economic and social boycott and was banished. Even in Madinah he was slandered and harassed by the combined forces of the Quraysh, the Jews and the hypocrites. But he left us the best example of sacrifice and forbearance, which Allah has asked us to follow:

لَّقَدْ كَانَ لَكُمْ فِي رَسُولِ ٱللَّهِ أُسْوَةٌ حَسَنَةٌ … ﴿٢١﴾

You have indeed in the Messenger of Allah a beautiful pattern of (conduct).

(al-Aḥzāb 33: 21)

Sacrifice is the essential requirement to test the sincerity of our *Īmān*. The path of Islam is the path of struggle. We will not be left alone just by saying that we believe. We will be tested so as to establish whether our belief is superficial or rooted firm in our hearts and manifested in our actions. The Glorious Qur'ān mentions this fact in several places so that we should not be perturbed when these trials come and so that we remain steadfast in our *Īmān*:

أَحَسِبَ ٱلنَّاسُ أَن يُتْرَكُوٓا۟ أَن يَقُولُوٓا۟ ءَامَنَّا وَهُمْ لَا يُفْتَنُونَ ﴿٢﴾
وَلَقَدْ فَتَنَّا ٱلَّذِينَ مِن قَبْلِهِمْ ۖ فَلَيَعْلَمَنَّ ٱللَّهُ ٱلَّذِينَ صَدَقُوا۟
وَلَيَعْلَمَنَّ ٱلْكَٰذِبِينَ ﴿٣﴾

Do people think that they will be left alone on saying, "We believe", and that they will not be tested? • We did test those before them, and Allah will certainly know those who are true from those who are false.

(al-'Ankabūt 29: 2–3)

أَمْ حَسِبْتُمْ أَن تَدْخُلُوا۟ ٱلْجَنَّةَ وَلَمَّا يَأْتِكُم مَّثَلُ ٱلَّذِينَ خَلَوْا۟
مِن قَبْلِكُم ۖ مَّسَّتْهُمُ ٱلْبَأْسَآءُ وَٱلضَّرَّآءُ … ﴿٢١٤﴾

Do you think that you shall enter Paradise without such (trials) as came to those who passed away before you? They encountered suffering and adversity.

(al-Baqarah 2: 214)

أَمْ حَسِبْتُمْ أَن تَدْخُلُوا۟ ٱلْجَنَّةَ وَلَمَّا يَعْلَمِ ٱللَّهُ ٱلَّذِينَ جَـٰهَدُوا۟

مِنكُمْ وَيَعْلَمَ ٱلصَّـٰبِرِينَ ﴿١٤٢﴾

Do you think that you would enter Heaven without Allah testing those who fought hard (in His cause) and remained steadfast?

(Āl 'Imrān 3: 142)

Just as to purify gold it has to be put in a crucible and heated so that all its impurities are evaporated, similarly it is only by trial and tribulation that we shape and develop our personalities. Those who stay firm, persevere and strive hard receive Allah's Guidance and reward. Thus, only after going through severe trials, tests and untold sacrifices was Ibrāhīm (may the peace and blessings of Allah be upon him) granted the honour of "Leader of mankind":

۞ وَإِذِ ٱبْتَلَىٰٓ إِبْرَٰهِـۧمَ رَبُّهُۥ بِكَلِمَـٰتٍ فَأَتَمَّهُنَّ ۖ قَالَ إِنِّى

جَاعِلُكَ لِلنَّاسِ إِمَامًا ... ﴿١٢٤﴾

And remember that Ibrāhīm was tried by his Lord with certain commands, which he fulfilled. He said: "I will make you a Leader of mankind."

(al-Baqarah 2: 124)

What should we sacrifice? To start with we are asked to sacrifice our possessions – things which we love to own and collect. Gold and silver, houses and cars, clothes and jewellery, cattle and land – all of which are the possessions of this world. Then we love our families and ourselves. All of these are to be sacrificed in the way of Allah if need be:

يَـٰٓأَيُّهَا ٱلَّذِينَ ءَامَنُوا۟ هَلْ أَدُلُّكُمْ عَلَىٰ تِجَـٰرَةٍ تُنجِيكُم مِّنْ عَذَابٍ أَلِيمٍ ﴿١٠﴾

تُؤْمِنُونَ بِٱللَّهِ وَرَسُولِهِۦ وَتُجَـٰهِدُونَ فِى سَبِيلِ ٱللَّهِ بِأَمْوَٰلِكُمْ

وَأَنفُسِكُمْ ۚ ... ﴿١١﴾

O you who believe! Shall I lead you to bargain that which will save you from a grievous penalty? • That you believe in Allah and His Messenger and that you strive (your utmost) in the cause of Allah, with your property and your persons.

(al-Ṣaff 61: 10–11)

Much more difficult is the sacrifice of time. All *'Ibādah* require our commitment to find time to fulfil our obligations to Allah and our fellow human beings. Still more difficult is to forgo our own opinions and submit our ego to the dictates of the *Sharī'ah*. Customs and traditions sometime conflict with the clear injunctions of the *Sharī'ah*. We may have to overcome the bitterness of family and withstand pressures of society. It is only then that we really succeed in obeying Allah.

The sacrifice of a goat, sheep or camel is just symbolic. We see the innocent animal is firmly in our control and is prepared to die for the will of its Creator. Are we ready to sacrifice our lives, possessions, our inner desires and our ego? Are we willing to place ourselves like a helpless animal in the control of the will of our Creator? That is the real sacrifice. Otherwise each year *'Īd al-Aḍḥā* comes and we diligently sacrifice some animals and we feel satisfied when we have fulfilled our obligation – no doubt we have performed an act of *'Ibādah* for which we will be rewarded.

لَن يَنَالَ ٱللَّهَ لُحُومُهَا وَلَا دِمَآؤُهَا وَلَـٰكِن يَنَالُهُ ٱلتَّقْوَىٰ مِنكُمْ … ﴿٣٧﴾

But it is not the blood and flesh which reaches Allah, it is the Taqwā *(God-Consciousness) which reaches Him.*

(al-Ḥajj 22: 37)

Let us prepare ourselves for a life of sacrifice. Without making sacrifices we will not be able to start the revival of Islam. We should be ready to sacrifice our time, our wealth, our resources and our lives, our personal likes and dislikes. If we sincerely strive in Allah's way He will open His doors of success for us. This is His promise:

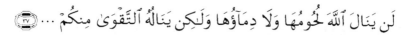

وَٱلَّذِينَ جَـٰهَدُوا۟ فِينَا لَنَهْدِيَنَّهُمْ سُبُلَنَا ۚ ... ﴿٦٩﴾

And those who strive in Our (cause) – We will certainly guide them to Our Paths.

(al-ʿAnkabūt 29: 69)

Together we can fulfil the obligation for which this *Ummah* is created. Without making sacrifices the revival of Islam will only remain a dream. This is the way to achieve Allah's pleasure. This is the way of the Prophets Ibrāhīm and Muḥammad (may peace and blessings of Allah be upon them), who proclaimed:

قُلْ إِنَّ صَلَاتِى وَنُسُكِى وَمَحْيَاىَ وَمَمَاتِى لِلَّهِ رَبِّ ٱلْعَـٰلَمِينَ ﴿١٦٢﴾

Truly, my prayer and my sacrifice, my life and my death are (all) for Allah, the Cherisher of the Worlds.

(al-Anʿām 6: 162)

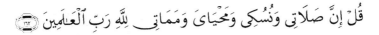

Hijrah

وَٱلَّذِينَ ءَامَنُواْ وَهَاجَرُواْ وَجَـٰهَدُواْ فِى سَبِيلِ ٱللَّهِ وَٱلَّذِينَ ءَاوَواْ
وَّنَصَرُوٓاْ أُوْلَـٰٓئِكَ هُمُ ٱلْمُؤْمِنُونَ حَقًّا ۚ لَّهُم مَّغْفِرَةٌ وَرِزْقٌ كَرِيمٌ ﴿٧٤﴾

Those who believe and migrate and fight for the cause of Allah as well as those who give (them) asylum and aid – they are the true believers. For them is forgiveness of sins and a provision most generous.

(al-Anfāl 8: 74)

It is narrated by Ḥārith al-Ash ʿarī that the Prophet (peace be upon him) said:

آمُرُكُمْ بِخَمْسٍ اللَّهُ أَمَرَنِي بِهِنَّ بِالْجَمَاعَةِ وَالسَّمْعِ وَالطَّاعَةِ وَالْهِجْرَةِ
وَالْجِهَادِ فِي سَبِيلِ اللَّهِ

(احمد)

I command you to perform five duties that Allah has ordered me to do. *Al-Samʿ* (listening attentively), and *al-Ṭāʿah* (obeying diligently), and *al-Hijrah* (migrating from evil society to a noble society), and *al-Jihād* (struggling in the way of Allah).

(Aḥmad)

By the mercy of Allah (*swt*) we have started the Islamic new year. We humbly pray that Allah may make this year one of peace and progress. May He shower His blessings and forgiveness on this *Ummah*. Without His help and without His support we cannot survive in this world.

As you know, the Islamic era starts with Hijrah (migration). This event does not commemorate either the birth or death of our Prophet (peace be upon him) nor does it celebrate the start of the Revelation. It was during the reign of ʿUmar (may Allah be pleased with him) that he decreed that the start of the Islamic era should be from the year of the migration of the Prophet (peace be upon him) from Makkah to Madinah. The Migration signifies the ascendancy of Islam and the establishment of an Islamic State. That was the decisive turn in the world history that changed its course for ever. This was the period when Islam overcame and subdued the forces of *Kufr* (disbelief).

But when we look back at the history of the period we see how the Prophet (peace be upon him) and his Companion, Abū Bakr (may Allah be pleased with him) had to leave Makkah in the dead of night to escape from the bloodthirsty clans of the Quraysh. Yet the Prophet (peace be upon him) was never desperate and dejected. He knew that Hijrah signified the dawn of the new era. During their journey to Madinah one of the emissaries of the Quraysh, Surāqah ibn Mālik, spotted them and was about to overtake them but his horse got stuck in the sand and he could not move. The Prophet (peace be upon him) asked Surāqah to accept Islam and predicted that I am seeing you wearing the gold bracelets of the King of Persia. He did not accept Islam at that time but promised that he would not inform the Quraysh about this encounter. Of course the prophecy came true when the Muslim army conquered Persia during the reign of ʿUmar ibn al-Khaṭṭāb (may Allah be pleased with him), and the gold bracelets of Kisrā were given to Surāqah. Indeed it was more than 1,400 years ago that Qādisiyah was conquered by Saʿd ibn Abī al-Waqqāṣ. History records the memorable encounter of the Muslim army with that of the Persians. That really was a glorious event in Islamic history. It was during this war that Saʿd ibn Abī al-Waqqāṣ sent Rabīʿah ibn ʿĀmir to Rustam, the commander of the Persian army. During his conversation with Rustam he uttered these profound words, which demonstrate very eloquently the purpose of this *Ummah*. He is reported to have said:

> Certainly God has chosen us so that through us those of His creation whom He so desires could be drawn away from the

worship of idols to *Tawḥīd*, from the narrow confines of preoccupation with this world to its boundless expanse and from the tyranny of rulers to the justice of Islam.

The *ḥadīth*, which was narrated at the start of this *Khuṭbah*, makes Hijrah obligatory for Muslims. So what is Hijrah? In Islamic terminology it can be defined as "leaving a place where it has become impossible to practice one's beliefs and thus moving to a place where *Īmān* can be safeguarded". Thus, it is in fact leaving the evil and turning to good. So in our life we should make a conscious effort to leave and abandon the path and the company of those who are transgressing Divine laws and migrate towards a good and righteous society.

It is instructive to reflect that the last month of the Islamic calendar commemorates the supreme act of submisson of the Prophet Ibrāhīm (peace be upon him). He was asked to sacrifice his only son, and he fulfilled this. The first month of the Islamic calendar unlike the New Year's days of other nations is not generally a joyous occasion. It is more sombre and in many ways a month of mourning. We remember the sacrifices that the Companions of the Prophet endured when they migrated. We remember the tragedy of Karbala where the grandson of the Prophet (peace be upon him) along with his close relations were martyred. He revolted against tyranny, against a system that was destroying the right of the people to elect their rulers. His courage and his sacrifice still evokes admiration and gives us the strength and conviction that we should be ready to face the armies of evil against all odds. As the Holy Qur'ān says:

وَلَا تَقُولُواْ لِمَن يُقۡتَلُ فِي سَبِيلِ ٱللَّهِ أَمۡوَٰتُۢۚ بَلۡ أَحۡيَآءٞ
وَلَٰكِن لَّا تَشۡعُرُونَ ١٥٤

And say not of those who are slain in the way of Allah: "They are dead." Nay they are living though you perceive it not.
(al-Baqarah 2: 154)

So the start of the New Year as well as the end of the year both remind us that our life should be a life of sacrifice.

The tenth day of Muḥarram is called *Yawm al-'Āshūrah*. This day has a very important significance apart from the martyrdom of Ḥusain (may Allah be pleased with him). According to certain *aḥādīth* this was the day when Adam (peace be upon him) was sent down to earth, Nūḥ's Ark rested on Mount Judi, Mūsā (peace be upon him) and his nation were saved from Pharaoh. Even the Quraysh used to fast and put new coverings on the Ka'bah on this day. Fasting on this day is the *Sunnah* of the Prophet.

It is narrated by Ibn al-'Abbās (may Allah be pleased with him) that when the Prophet came to Madinah he saw that the Jews were fasting on *Yawm al-'Āshūrah*. He enquired of them why do they so fast? They replied that it represented the great day when Mūsā (peace be upon him) and his nation were saved and Pharaoh drowned. Mūsā (peace be upon him) kept a fast on this day as a thanksgiving and hence his example was followed. Then the Prophet advised them that Muslims were closer to Mūsā than they and that he fasted and asked others to fast as well (Bukhārī and Muslim). To keep the distinct identity of Muslims, the Prophet said that they should fast on two days, either on the 9th and 10th or the 10th and 11th of Muḥarram.

Let us pray that Allah may give us courage to follow the examples of the Companions to abandon the pleasure of our homes and prepare ourselves for Hijrah and Jihād. We should also follow the examples of the Prophets Ibrāhīm and Muḥammad (peace be upon them) and Ḥusain ibn 'Alī (may Allah be pleased with him) and prepare ourselves for the sacrifice of our time, money and lives if required for the sake of Allah (*swt*). (*Āmīn.*)

Jihād fī Sabīl Allāh

يَٰٓأَيُّهَا ٱلَّذِينَ ءَامَنُواْ هَلْ أَدُلُّكُمْ عَلَىٰ تِجَٰرَةٍ تُنجِيكُم مِّنْ عَذَابٍ أَلِيمٍ ﴿١٠﴾
تُؤْمِنُونَ بِٱللَّهِ وَرَسُولِهِۦ وَتُجَٰهِدُونَ فِى سَبِيلِ ٱللَّهِ بِأَمْوَٰلِكُمْ وَأَنفُسِكُمْ ۚ
ذَٰلِكُمْ خَيْرٌ لَّكُمْ إِن كُنتُمْ تَعْلَمُونَ ﴿١١﴾

O you who believe! Shall I lead you to a bargain that will save you from a grievous penalty? • That you believe in Allah and His Messenger and that you strive (your utmost) in the cause of Allah, with your property and your persons: that will be best for you, if you but knew!

(al-Ṣaff 61: 10–11)

Jihād is the most vilified word of the Islamic vocabulary by non-Muslims. It is commonly translated as "Holy War". The scenario it depicts is very well illustrated by Mawlana Mawdūdī (may Allah have mercy on him) in his book, *Jihād in Islam.* He writes:

> The word "Jihād" conjures up the vision of a marching band of religious fanatics with savage beards and fiery eyes brandishing drawn swords and attacking the infidels wherever they meet them and pressing them under the edge of the sword for the recital of *Kalimah.* Artists have drawn this picture with masterly strokes and have inscribed these words in bold letters: **The History of this Nation is a tale of Bloodshed.**

This graphic description is very familiar to us who live in the West. This is how the media portrays Islam. The cause of this misunderstanding, either innocently or wilfully, is that of ignoring the real Message of Islam for humanity. Islam is seen merely as a "religion" and Muslims are just another "nation".

Islam, as we know, is a complete code of life. It has its spiritual and moral dimensions. It also provides guidance in social, economic and political fields. By *Ṣalāh*, *Zakāh*, *Ṣawm* and *Ḥajj* it instructs its followers to submit completely to the will of Allah (*swt*). As we have seen all *'Ibādah* prescribed by Islam are performed collectively. They lead to the development of the individual within a God-conscious and law-abiding society. This means that we cannot fulfil all our obligations even if we have the freedom to pray, fast and perform *Ḥajj* when other parts of the Islamic *Shari'āh* are not implemented by the society and more particularly by the state. In Islam, sovereignty belongs to Allah (*swt*). All corruption in society begins when man assumes the lordship. Whether it is a dictatorial form of government or a democratic one, if people have the freedom to legislate disregarding the laws given by Allah (*swt*) it will lead to injustice and corruption.

The other fact is that Muslims are not a racial, linguistic, geographic or national group. Anyone, whatever his origin, can become a Muslim by accepting the sovereignty of Allah and following the Guidance brought by His Messengers.

Jihād literary means to struggle to the utmost or to exert one's utmost endeavour in promoting a cause. The avoidance in this context of other Arabic words like *Ḥarb* (war) and *Qitāl* (fighting) for this struggle is deliberate, because Jihād is not only war but has several other dimensions that we will discuss later. The other fact to be noted is that Jihād is not just any struggle; it is "a struggle in the cause of Allah". This means all deeds are undertaken with sincerity to gain the pleasure of Allah and not with any other motive.

The first and foremost struggle one has to face daily in submitting to the will of Allah (*swt*) is against one's own self. There are many commandments from Allah that we are required to follow. For example, if we fail to get up for *Fajr* Prayers, as we prefer not to leave our warm beds, or if we neglect our duties to others as we are preoccupied with our own affairs, then struggle against oneself is Jihād. Another aspect would be if we see our family and friends disobeying the commands of Allah or starting innovations that are against the *Sharīʿah*, and we meekly accept the pressure of our corrupt society and do not raise our voice against them nor do we try to stop them, whereas the Prophet said:

مَنْ رَأَى مُنْكَرًا فَلْيُغَيِّرْهُ بِيَدِهِ وَمَنْ لَمْ يَسْتَطِعْ فَبِلِسَانِهِ وَمَنْ لَمْ يَسْتَطِعْ فَبِقَلْبِهِ وَذَلِكَ أَضْعَفُ الإِيمَانِ

(مسلم)

Whoever amongst you sees an evil he should try to change it by his hands (i.e. using force) and if he cannot do that he should use his tongue (to condemn it). And if he has not that much courage at least he should realise in his heart that it is bad and this is the lowest stage of *Īmān*.

(Muslim)

Sadly, some of us just remain on the lowest stage of *Īmān*. But *Amr bil Maʿrūf* (calling people to righteousness) and *Nahī ʿanil Munkar* (stopping people from doing evil) are compulsory on us. We need this intellectual and missionary zeal that requires us to convey the Message of Islam to the wider society. Maybe we avoid this important duty because it can lead to opposition and ridicule from others. But this is the *Sunnah* of all Prophets (peace be upon them all). They candidly conveyed the Message without any fear for their safety. Indeed, they were all bitterly opposed by their own kith and kin and their friends. But regardless of such fierce opposition, that many a time became very violent, they were not deterred from their mission. This Jihād (struggle) is part of the Prophetic mission. This is the way we are required to follow.

Sayyid Quṭb Shahīd (may Allah have mercy on him) in his monumental *Tafsīr, Fī Ẓilāl al-Qur'ān,* has quoted Imām Ibn Qayyim al-Jawziyyah, who in his famous book *Zād al-Maʿād* wrote a chapter about the *Sīrah* of the Prophet (peace be upon him). In this, he described in detail the Prophet's dealings with unbelievers and hypocrites from his Prophethood until his death. The following represents a summary of what he wrote:

> The first Revelation that came to the Prophet (peace be upon him) asked him to recite in the name of your Lord. At that time, he was not asked to propagate his mission widely. Then, after some time, this *āyah* of *Sūrah al-Muddaththir* was revealed:
>
> يَـٰٓأَيُّهَا ٱلْمُدَّثِّرُ ۝١ قُمْ فَأَنذِرْ ۝٢
>
> *O you wrapped up (in a mantle)! Arise and deliver the warning.*
>
> (al-Muddaththir 74: 1–2)
>
> At that stage, he climbed up Mount Ṣafā and called all the inhabitants of Makkah and warned his relations and his nation. To start the work of *Da'wah* the Prophet (peace be upon him) devoted himself to preaching and persuading people. He did not use any force. He was asked to be forgiving and to patiently bear the violence used against him and his followers.
>
> After several years of *Da'wah*, when no headway could be made in persuading the Quraysh to accept Islam, the Prophet (peace be upon him) was given permission to migrate to Madinah. In Madinah, he was given permission to defend the Islamic State against aggressions from the Quraysh.
>
> Finally, when the Quraysh broke the Treaty of Hudabiyah, the Prophet (peace be upon him) was permitted to wage war against those who rejected the Treaty. When this command came there were three possible relationships with non-Muslims prevailing: people who signed the covenant of peace, people who were belligerents and those who sought protection from the Islamic State.

This is a summary of Ibn Qayyim's narration that illustrates the Islamic methodology behind Jihād. Islam gives everyone the choice of accepting Islam or rejecting it. Armed struggle is only against those who impose their sovereignty over others and who prevent their subjects from accepting Islam.

Thus, the training we receive from all *'Ibādah* should prepare us for Jihād (struggle) against our own self, family, society and if needs be the state. This duty is emphasised in several places in the Holy Qur'ān:

إِنَّمَا ٱلْمُؤْمِنُونَ ٱلَّذِينَ ءَامَنُوا۟ بِٱللَّهِ وَرَسُولِهِۦ ثُمَّ لَمْ يَرْتَابُوا۟
وَجَـٰهَدُوا۟ بِأَمْوَٰلِهِمْ وَأَنفُسِهِمْ فِى سَبِيلِ ٱللَّهِ ۚ أُو۟لَـٰٓئِكَ هُمُ
ٱلصَّـٰدِقُونَ ﴿١٥﴾

Only those are believers who believe in Allah and His Messenger, and have never since doubted, but have striven with their belongings and their persons in the cause of Allah: such are the sincere ones.
(al-Ḥujurāt 49: 15)

هُوَ ٱلَّذِىٓ أَرْسَلَ رَسُولَهُۥ بِٱلْهُدَىٰ وَدِينِ ٱلْحَقِّ لِيُظْهِرَهُۥ عَلَى ٱلدِّينِ
كُلِّهِۦ وَلَوْ كَرِهَ ٱلْمُشْرِكُونَ ﴿٩﴾ يَـٰٓأَيُّهَا ٱلَّذِينَ ءَامَنُوا۟ هَلْ أَدُلُّكُمْ عَلَىٰ تِجَـٰرَةٍ
تُنجِيكُم مِّنْ عَذَابٍ أَلِيمٍ ﴿١٠﴾ تُؤْمِنُونَ بِٱللَّهِ وَرَسُولِهِۦ وَتُجَـٰهِدُونَ فِى
سَبِيلِ ٱللَّهِ بِأَمْوَٰلِكُمْ وَأَنفُسِكُمْ ۚ ذَٰلِكُمْ خَيْرٌ لَّكُمْ إِن كُنتُمْ تَعْلَمُونَ ﴿١١﴾

It is He Who has sent His Messenger with Guidance and the Dīn *of Truth that it may proclaim over all ways of life even though unbelievers may detest (it) • O you who believe! Shall I lead you to a bargain that will save you from a grievous penalty • that you believe in Allah and His Messenger, and that you strive to your utmost* (Jihād) *in the cause of Allah with your property and your persons: that will be best for you.*
(al-Ṣaff 61: 9–11)

إِنَّ ٱللَّهَ ٱشۡتَرَىٰ مِنَ ٱلۡمُؤۡمِنِينَ أَنفُسَهُمۡ وَأَمۡوَٰلَهُم بِأَنَّ لَهُمُ
ٱلۡجَنَّةَۚ يُقَٰتِلُونَ فِي سَبِيلِ ٱللَّهِ فَيَقۡتُلُونَ وَيُقۡتَلُونَۖ وَعۡدًا عَلَيۡهِ
حَقّٗا فِي ٱلتَّوۡرَىٰةِ وَٱلۡإِنجِيلِ وَٱلۡقُرۡءَانِۚ وَمَنۡ أَوۡفَىٰ بِعَهۡدِهِۦ مِنَ
ٱللَّهِۚ فَٱسۡتَبۡشِرُواْ بِبَيۡعِكُمُ ٱلَّذِي بَايَعۡتُم بِهِۦۚ وَذَٰلِكَ هُوَ
ٱلۡفَوۡزُ ٱلۡعَظِيمُ ١١١

Allah has purchased of the believers their persons and their goods; for theirs (in return) is the garden (of Paradise): They fight in His cause and slay and are slain. This is a promise binding on Him in Truth through the Tawrāt, the Injīl and the Qur'ān. And who is more faithful to his covenant than Allah? Then rejoice in the bargain, which you have concluded: that is the achievement supreme.

(al-Tawbah 9: 111)

Let us resolve to proclaim the truth of Islam with our utmost efforts. Let us prepare ourselves to sacrifice our belongings and our lives for the sake of this *Dīn*. There are great and untold rewards for those who die in the cause of Allah. (*Āmīn.*)

Da'wah

وَلۡتَكُن مِّنكُمۡ أُمَّةٞ يَدۡعُونَ إِلَى ٱلۡخَيۡرِ وَيَأۡمُرُونَ بِٱلۡمَعۡرُوفِ وَيَنۡهَوۡنَ عَنِ
ٱلۡمُنكَرِۚ وَأُوْلَٰٓئِكَ هُمُ ٱلۡمُفۡلِحُونَ ١٠٤

Let there arise out of you a band of people inviting to all that is good, enjoining what is right, and forbidding what is wrong: they are the ones to attain success.

(Āl 'Imrān 3: 104)

Allah (*swt*) has given us the ability to know what is good and what is evil. We instinctively like goodness and dislike evil. But this primary instinct is not sufficient to guide us in the very many complex aspects of our life on this earth. Hence, in His Mercy He has sent down Messengers with clear Guidance to help us live our lives in peace and harmony.

This is also necessary because we are accountable for our conduct to Allah (*swt*) on the Day of Judgement. We could plead ignorance if we did not know what the Right Path was. This is explained in the Holy Qur'ān as follows:

رُّسُلٗا مُّبَشِّرِينَ وَمُنذِرِينَ لِئَلَّا يَكُونَ لِلنَّاسِ عَلَى ٱللَّهِ حُجَّةُۢ بَعۡدَ
ٱلرُّسُلِۚ وَكَانَ ٱللَّهُ عَزِيزًا حَكِيمٗا ١٦٥

Messengers who gave tidings as well as warnings that humankind, after (the coming) of the Messengers, should have no plea against Allah: For Allah is Exalted in Power, Wise.

(al-Nisā' 4: 165)

Each Messenger was sent to his own people so that he would explain the Message to them in their own language. But the Prophethood of Muḥammad (peace be upon him) was twofold. He was sent down to the people of Arabia as well as to all humankind. As he was the last Prophet and Messenger, the responsibility for conveying the Message of Allah to all humanity till the end of time rests on this *Ummah*:

وَكَذَٰلِكَ جَعَلْنَٰكُمْ أُمَّةً وَسَطًا لِّتَكُونُوا۟ شُهَدَآءَ عَلَى ٱلنَّاسِ
وَيَكُونَ ٱلرَّسُولُ عَلَيْكُمْ شَهِيدًا ... ﴿١٤٣﴾

Thus have We made you an Ummah *justly balanced, that you might be witness over the nations and the Messenger a witness over yourselves.*

(al-Baqarah 2: 143)

Thus, to protect the Message and its continuous propagation, Allah (*swt*) has undertaken two vital steps: first, that the Holy Qur'ān will be preserved from corruption till eternity. Allah says in *Sūrah al-Ḥijr*:

إِنَّا نَحْنُ نَزَّلْنَا ٱلذِّكْرَ وَإِنَّا لَهُۥ لَحَٰفِظُونَ ﴿٩﴾

We have, without doubt, sent down the Message; and We will assuredly guard it (from corruption).

(al-Ḥijr 15: 9)

Second, there will always be at least one group in this *Ummah* that will stand firm on *Dīn* and convey the Message of Truth.

Thus, *Da'wah* is not just one of the many good deeds to be undertaken but it is rather the prime responsibility of this *Ummah*:

كُنتُمْ خَيْرَ أُمَّةٍ أُخْرِجَتْ لِلنَّاسِ تَأْمُرُونَ بِٱلْمَعْرُوفِ وَتَنْهَوْنَ
عَنِ ٱلْمُنكَرِ وَتُؤْمِنُونَ بِٱللَّهِ ... ﴿١١٠﴾

You are the best of peoples, evolved for mankind, enjoining what is right, forbidding what is wrong and believing in Allah.

(Āl 'Imrān 3: 110)

In the process of *Da'wah* there are three factors involved: The Message (*Da'wah*); The Messenger (*Dā'ī*) and The Addressee (*Mad'ū*).

What is the Message? A very simplistic way to say this is to become a true Muslim. What is the difference between being a Muslim and becoming a Muslim? "Being a Muslim" indicates self-satisfied passivity whereas "becoming a Muslim" shows the dynamic and ceaseless struggle. Becoming a Muslim has two implications: First, to invite oneself to surrender to the will of Allah (*swt*). As explained in the Qur'ān:

وَمَنْ أَحْسَنُ قَوْلًا مِّمَّن دَعَآ إِلَى ٱللَّهِ وَعَمِلَ صَٰلِحًا وَقَالَ
إِنَّنِى مِنَ ٱلْمُسْلِمِينَ ﴿٣٣﴾

Who is better in speech than one who calls (others) to Allah, works righteousness, and says, "I am of those who bow in Islam."
(Fuṣṣilat 41: 33)

Second, to invite the whole of society to live in submission to the will of Allah (*swt*). These two processes continue simultaneously.

Who is the Messenger? Every Muslim is a *Dā'ī.* You have to try and change your personality to adopt the character of *Dā'ī* in your daily life. Some people say that if we ourselves are sinners how can we invite others to goodness? Imām Ghazālī in his famous work *Iḥyā' al-'Ulūm al-Dīn* discusses this very issue in the Chapter on "*Amr bil Mar'ūf wan-Nahī 'anil Munkar.*" He raises this question: How can a person who drinks and is a transgressor (*Fāsiq*) do *Da'wah*? Can he ask others not to drink? Imām Ghazālī explains there are two commandments. First, the prohibition of drinking. Second, stopping others from drinking. By not following the first order he is not absolved of his responsibility to carry out the other. Just as one who does not fast should not miss his Prayers, as they are two different commandments.

Some people make an excuse that they are not learned enough to do *Da'wah.* The Prophet (peace be upon him) has asked us to "convey from me, even if it is one *āyah*". On the occasion of his last *Ḥajj* he told the assembled Companions to convey his Message to those who were not present here. Thus, we see from the lives of the *Ṣaḥābah* that they conveyed this Message to the farthest corners of the earth.

Who is the addressee? Everyone is a potential Muslim. Thus, there are 55 million in this country. Each individual is different. Hence, you should approach him in an appropriate manner. ʿAli ibn Abī Ṭālib (may Allah be pleased with him) has made a very perceptive remark. You should try to remember this. He said: "There are desires and inclinations in peoples' hearts. Sometimes they are ready to listen and sometimes they are not. Try to enter hearts when they are inclined to listen, because the affairs of hearts are such that if they are forced they become blind and refuse to accept."

Thus, we have to know the psychology of our addressees. It is essential that we respect their feelings and avoid hurting their dear and emotional attachments. Then there are different aspects of the same thing. You should try to follow the easy way. It is narrated about the Prophet (peace be upon him) that if there were two options open to him he always chose the easy one. You have to choose the appropriate time and place to present your message. Of course the message has to be varied according to the competence of the addressee. If you see people are getting bored you should stop. If someone argues do not try to win the argument thus humiliating him. Stop and give him time to think.

You should realise that *Daʿwah* is a long and tiring process. You can not achieve success very quickly. It needs lots of patience and perseverance. Even then it may not bring any result. Thus, people often give up in despair. But you should realise that your responsibility is only to convey and you cannot change peoples' hearts if they do not want change to themselves. It is only Allah (*swt*) who can give Guidance to whom He wishes. If you study the lives of the Prophets you will see many of them failed to change the hearts of their own family. Nūḥ (peace be upon him) preached for 950 years yet even his wife and his son did not accept Islam. So the father of Ibrāhīm, wife of Lūṭ and Abū Ṭālib, uncle of the Prophet, remained unaccepting of Islam.

Let us pray that Allah (*swt*) may make us realise our duty of conveying *Daʿwah* and give us *Īmān* and courage so that we take up this task. (*Āmīn.*)

How to Study the Qur'ān

وَلَقَدۡ يَسَّرۡنَا ٱلۡقُرۡءَانَ لِلذِّكۡرِ فَهَلۡ مِن مُّدَّكِرٖ ١٧

And We have indeed made the Qur'ān easy to understand and remember: then is there any that will receive admonition?
(al-Qamar 54: 17)

The Glorious Qur'ān is a Book of Guidance and the mercy of Allah (*swt*) for mankind. We usually say that the Qur'ān is a Book. Certainly it is collected and put together between two covers, but it is much more than a mere book. So how does al-Qur'ān describe itself. Unlike any other book that I know of, the Qur'ān has used more than fifty adjectives to explain what it is. Some of these are as follows:

Exhortation, Warning, Guidance, Enlightenment, Inner insight, Clear way, Healing for (the diseases) of the heart, Mercy, Convincing proof, Clear statement, Criterion for right and wrong, Clear proof, Remembrance, Not crooked, Straight and clear book, Blessed, Glorious, The Book, The Scripture and of course, al-Qur'ān.

Thus, we see it is much more than a book. It may be considered as a book of reference, a manual and a guide that should be our constant companion to lead us to the Right Path in the journey of our lives.

Ustādh Khurram Murad in his book, *The Way to the Qur'ān*, has given valuable advice on studying the Holy Qur'ān. I will try to summarise what he has written:

- There are certain prerequisites that we should fulfil for receiving the blessings of the Qur'ān. The first requirement is that we should realise that the Qur'ān does not open its treasures of wisdom for those who have no faith in its Divine origin. Thus, to receive guidance from the Qur'ān we should have a strong and deep Faith that the Qur'ān is the Word of Allah (*swt*).

- Second, we should approach it with purity of intention and purpose. The purpose should be to seek guidance from the Qur'ān. Some people have pre-conceived ideas and they approach the Qur'ān to corroborate their own views. They try to read their own ideas into the Qur'ān. Thus, instead of receiving Guidance they get what they were looking for. We should approach the Qur'ān in deep humility with an open mind seeking Allah's help to receive Guidance.
- Third, we should be grateful to Allah (*swt*) for giving us this blessed Book. The more grateful we are the more the mercy of Allah will engulf us.
- Fourth, having accepted the Qur'ān as the Book of Allah, we should open our hearts and accept everything mentioned in the Qur'ān as true and have complete faith in it.
- Finally, it is a Book that changed the history of mankind forever. When we approach it we should be ready to obey its commandments and prepare to change our lifestyle and show the readiness to comply with its guidance. Only then will we receive the blessings of the Qur'ān. Thus, there are very many non-Muslims, for example Orientalists, who have spent their lives in the study of the Qur'ān but they have failed to receive any guidance from it because they do not fulfil these requirements.

Studying the Qur'ān on your own poses some problems. Some *'ulamā'* discourage novices from undertaking any study of the Qur'ān on their own. They say the Qur'ān is difficult for a lay person to understand. It is only for the *'ulamā'* to explain its meaning. But this argument runs counter to the teachings of the Qur'ān. Again, historical evidence we obtain from the lives of the *Ṣaḥābah* (may Allah be pleased with them) shows that they all were able to benefit from the teachings of the Qur'ān. As we know, they were not all scholars. They were people from all walks of life and they were able to understand the meaning of the Qur'ān and follow its guidance.

There are two levels of study and understanding. One is called *Tadhakkur* which means admonition, advice, remembrance, taking heed or taking to heart. This primary level is easy for everyone to understand and practice. Indeed the Holy Qur'ān itself has repeatedly asserted this in *Sūrah al-Qamar*:

وَلَقَدْ يَسَّرْنَا ٱلْقُرْءَانَ لِلذِّكْرِ فَهَلْ مِن مُّدَّكِرٍ ﴿١٧﴾

And We have indeed made the Qur'ān easy to understand and remember: Then is there any that will receive admonition?
(al-Qamar 54: 17, 22, 32 and 40)

The other more advanced level is called *Tadabbur* which means reflection, deep thought and full comprehension. This may not be possible for everyone to achieve. But the Qur'ān urges its readers to attempt this as well:

أَفَلَا يَتَدَبَّرُونَ ٱلْقُرْءَانَ أَمْ عَلَىٰ قُلُوبٍ أَقْفَالُهَآ ﴿٢٤﴾

Do they not earnestly seek to reflect on the Qur'ān, or are their hearts locked up by them?
(Muḥammad 47: 24)

Of course when you are studying the Qur'ān there are certain risks, which you should be aware of. First, you should know your own limitations. You should evaluate your own knowledge of Arabic, *Ḥadīth* and *Sīrah*. If you do not know Arabic you have to rely on translations.

Second, each subject has its own vocabulary hence you should know basic keywords of the Qur'ān, for example, *Ilāh, Rabb, Dīn, Taqwā, 'Ibādah*, etc. There are now some dictionaries of Qur'ānic terms available in English as well that will help you in your study.

This brings me to the third point, that you should read the whole Qur'ān with a translation and if possible with some reliable *tafsīr* once. This will help you to understand the overall message of the Qur'ān. It is essential that you should always confine your own conclusions so as to confirm with *tafsīr* and the *'ulamā'*.

Fourth, the Qur'ān is a vast and multi-dimensional work. It will take years to understand it fully. Thus, do not attempt to derive your own *Fiqh* from it and do not go beyond the general consensus of the *Ummah*. It may be that sometimes you do not understand the complete meaning of the passage by studying on your own. Group study and mutual discussion are often helpful. You may also seek the help of an *'Ālim*.

And finally, we are accustomed to reading books that present information, ideas and arguments systematically and coherently. So when we embark on the study of the Qur'ān, we expect that this book will revolve around a definite subject. However when we open the Qur'ān we encounter a completely unfamiliar genre of literature. We notice that it embodies precepts of belief and conduct, moral injunctions, good tidings, dire warnings, stories of past nations, signs of Allah visible in the Universe and so on. It also deals with cultural, social, political and legal issues. These are discussed in a different way unlike the way books on social sciences deal with these issues. As we are not accustomed to this we sometimes become confused.

We should realise that the subject of the Qur'ān is *man* and that it seeks to explain the ultimate cause of man's success and failure. The Qur'ān is the Book of Guidance, thus, it confines itself to essentials and its contents revolve around this theme. We should also know that the style of the Qur'ān is oratorical and not narrative. As you know, oral language and style differ greatly from one written composition to another. Therefore, literal translations of the Qur'ān lack literary force, fluency, eloquence and charm. Thus, if you try to understand the Qur'ān through translations you may be disappointed.

If you keep in mind these important differences between other books and the Glorious Qur'ān, you will understand its logical arrangement, its rhetorical force and rhythmic beauty which penetrates human hearts.

I hope this brief introduction and the guidelines so delineated will help you to start on your own lifetime journey of reading and understanding the Divine Book. May Allah (*swt*) help us all to derive benefit from His Book and may we receive its blessings. (*Āmīn.*)

The *Sunnah*

مَّن يُطِعِ ٱلرَّسُولَ فَقَدۡ أَطَاعَ ٱللَّهَ ... ﴿٨٠﴾

He who obeys the Messenger, obeys Allah.
(al-Nisā' 4: 80)

قُلۡ إِن كُنتُمۡ تُحِبُّونَ ٱللَّهَ فَٱتَّبِعُونِي يُحۡبِبۡكُمُ ٱللَّهُ وَيَغۡفِرۡ لَكُمۡ
ذُنُوبَكُمۡۗ وَٱللَّهُ غَفُورٞ رَّحِيمٞ ﴿٣١﴾

Say: "If you do love Allah, follow me: Allah will love you and forgive your sins. For Allah is Oft-Forgiving, Most Merciful."
(Āl 'Imrān 3: 31)

لَّقَدۡ كَانَ لَكُمۡ فِي رَسُولِ ٱللَّهِ أُسۡوَةٌ حَسَنَةٞ لِّمَن كَانَ يَرۡجُواْ
ٱللَّهَ وَٱلۡيَوۡمَ ٱلۡأٓخِرَ وَذَكَرَ ٱللَّهَ كَثِيرٗا ﴿٢١﴾

You have indeed in the Messenger of Allah a beautiful pattern of conduct for anyone whose hope is in Allah and the Final Day, and who engages much in the praise of Allah.
(al-Aḥzāb 33: 21)

After the Holy Qur'ān, the *Sunnah* (practice) of the Prophet (peace be upon him) is the second most important source of the *Sharī'ah*. *Aḥādīth* are the record of the *Sunnah*. Usually, people use *ḥadīth* and *Sunnah* interchangeably. However, this is not the case. There is a slight difference in their meanings. The literal meaning of *ḥadīth* is news, information and communication. Its technical definition is speech or acts of the Prophet (peace be upon him). It also includes those acts that were performed in his presence and which he did not disapprove of. Thus, by his silence he gave them his tacit approval.

Unlike the Qur'ān, *ḥadīth* literature is not composed of one corpus. It is based on individual narrations by different Companions of the Prophet (peace be upon him). With the passage of time however, some unscrupulous people tried to invent false *aḥādīth*. To combat this menace, the *Muḥaddaithūn* have taken great pains to devise a science of *Asmā' al-Rijāl* that contains the biographical details of all narrators of *aḥādīth*. This identifies those who are reliable from those who are cheats. *Aḥādīth* in this respect then, have been classified into the following three categories:

A *Ṣaḥīḥ ḥadīth* is the most authentic *ḥadīth*. It requires an unbroken chain of reliable narrators who narrate it and its contents perfectly.

Ḥasan literally means beautiful or sound. It is an *ḥadīth* that contains some minor defects in the chain of narrators or in the text.

Ḍa'īf literally means weak. It is a *ḥadīth* that consists of serious defects in its narration and/or text. It may be acceptable however, if it is supported by *Ṣaḥīḥ* and *Ḥasan aḥādīth*.

Fabricated and false *aḥādīth* are called *Mawḍū'*. These should be avoided. Unfortunately, unguarded preachers use them to embellish their talks.

Thus, when you study *aḥādīth* you should be aware of these different categories.

The literal meaning of *Sunnah* is a clear way, a well-trodden path, a levelled path and from this it has come to mean traditions, principles and customs. This word is used several times in the Qur'ān in its primary meaning:

فَلَن تَجِدَ لِسُنَّتِ ٱللَّهِ تَبۡدِيلًاۖ وَلَن تَجِدَ لِسُنَّتِ ٱللَّهِ تَحۡوِيلًا ﴿٤٣﴾

You shall never find any change in Allah's Sunnah *and you will never find any alternation in Allah's* Sunnah.

(Fāṭir 35: 43)

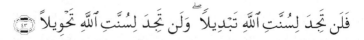

The Holy Qur'ān has laid down basic principles whilst the *Sunnah* provides precise details. The Qur'ān is the manual and the *Sunnah* is the practical demonstration. As you cannot learn to drive by reading a driving manual, you need practical lessons to master the art of driving. Similarly, you cannot practice Islam just by reading the Holy Qur'ān. The basis of the *Sunnah* is the practical example which the Companions learned from the Prophet. He told them "you pray as you see me praying". The Companions taught the *Tābi'ūn*, the succeeding generation, and they taught the next. Just as the Qur'ān is the verbal transmission of Allah's words, the *Sunnah* is the practical demonstration of the way that the Prophet conducted his life. Both the narration of the Qur'ān and the practice of the *Sunnah* are continuously preserved by the *Ummah*. The Prophet (peace be upon him) said:

عَلَيْكُمْ بِسُنَّتِي وَسُنَّةِ الْخُلَفَاءِ الرَّاشِدِينَ الْمَهْدِيِّينَ

(أبو داود والترمذي)

> It is obligatory on you to follow my *Sunnah* and the *Sunnah* of my Rightly-Guided *Khulafā'* (successors).
> (Abū Dā'ūd and Tirmidhī)

We see differences in the way people pray. Which is the correct and right way? The answer is, all are correct and right because all follow the *Sunnah* of the Prophet (peace be upon him) and *Sunnah* can be different. It is our tragedy that we do not understand that all these differences in minor detail are there because the Prophet (peace be upon him) allowed such variations. For example, after the last *Ḥajj* people came to the Prophet (peace be upon him) and said they did this ritual before that or they did something else differently and the Prophet kept on saying it is all right. In other words, there is no shortcoming in your *Ḥajj*. There are a great many narrations about *Tashahhud*. All traditions are narrated by eminent *Ṣaḥābah*. If I follow the one narrated by 'Abdullāh ibn Mas'ūd and someone else follows the one narrated by 'Abdullāh ibn 'Umar and yet another follows the narration of *Ummul Mu'minīn* 'Ā'ishah (may Allah be pleased with them), who is to say which one is right? All of them relate it from the Prophet (peace be upon him).

I will encourage you to read *aḥādīth* so that you enrich yourselves with the wisdom of the Prophet (peace be upon him) and follow his path. Nonetheless you will need some guidance in this respect:

There are six particularly authentic collections of *aḥādīth*. In Arabic they are called the *Ṣiḥāḥ Sittah*. These books were compiled by eminent scholars of *ḥadīth* after painstaking research. They being Imām Bukhārī, Imām Muslim, Imām Abū Dā'ūd, Imām Tirmidhī, Imām Nasā'ī, and Imām Ibn Mājah. *Al-Muwaṭṭa'* of Imām Mālik is also considered to be one of the most authentic collections. It will be difficult for you to embark on studying such massive works at the outset. However, if you want to choose any from this list you will find *Ṣaḥīḥ Muslim* the easiest to study as its arrangement is very simple. It brings together all the *aḥādīth* on one topic under one heading. However, for beginners it is better to start with selections from these books. Here, *Riyāḍ al-Ṣāliḥīn* by Imām Nawawī is very good for beginners. His *Forty Ḥadīth* is also very handy. If you are more ambitious you may read *Mishkāt al-Maṣābiḥ,* a selection compiled by Walīuddīn Muḥammad ibn ʿAbdullāh al-Khaṭīb al-Tabrīzī in three volumes. English translations of all these selections are available.

When you are studying *ḥadīth* you should remember the following five principles:

First, the Qur'ān should be the real criteria. Two names of the Qur'ān are *al-Furqān* and *al-Muhaymin,* both meaning criteria on which everything has to be judged. A *ḥadīth* should not be in contradiction with the Qur'ānic injunction.

Second, one single *ḥadīth* is a part of the whole corpus of *aḥādīth*. Unless you read all *aḥādīth* on one topic, a single *ḥadīth* may sometimes be difficult to interpret on its own.

Third, the language of *ḥadīth* as you know is Arabic. If you do not know Arabic, you have to rely on translations. But translations do not always convey the accurate meaning.

Fourth, a *ḥadīth* records the saying or the act of the Prophet (peace be upon him) as said or done in a specific context. If you try to generalise from one *ḥadīth* then you will be misled. Those of you who have studied logic will know the pitfalls of this form of argument. Take for example this *ḥadīth*:

أُمِرْتُ أَنْ أُقَاتِلَ النَّاسَ حَتَّى يَشْهَدُوا أَنْ لاَ إِلَهَ إِلاَّ اللَّهُ وَأَنَّ مُحَمَّدًا رَسُولُ اللَّهِ

(متفق عليه)

I have been ordered to fight against the people until they testify that there is no god but Allah and that Muḥammad is the Messenger of Allah.
(Bukhārī and Muslim)

If we do not know in which context and about which group of people this was said and you try to generalise that it is obligatory to fight against all non-Muslims then the accusation of Orientalists will be correct, namely that Islam was spread by the force of the sword.

Finally, *Dīn* is based on wisdom and *Fiṭrah* meaning nature. Both the Qur'ān and the *Sunnah* are based on reason. Hence, all authentic *aḥādīth* should also be based on reason. This does not mean that if you cannot understand any *Ṣaḥīḥ ḥadīth* you should reject it. Like any other branch of knowledge only those who are expert in their field know the exact implications of the text in question.

I hope this very brief introduction will help you to appreciate the necessity of learning from the *aḥādīth* the wisdom of the Prophet (peace be upon him). May Allah help you towards a proper understanding of His *Dīn*. (*Āmīn*.)

Fiqh

وَمَا كَانَ ٱلْمُؤْمِنُونَ لِيَنفِرُوا۟ كَآفَّةً ۚ فَلَوْلَا نَفَرَ مِن كُلِّ فِرْقَةٍ
مِّنْهُمْ طَآئِفَةٌ لِّيَتَفَقَّهُوا۟ فِى ٱلدِّينِ وَلِيُنذِرُوا۟ قَوْمَهُمْ إِذَا
رَجَعُوٓا۟ إِلَيْهِمْ لَعَلَّهُمْ يَحْذَرُونَ ﴿١٢٢﴾

Nor should the Believers all go forth together. If a contingent from every expedition remained behind, they could devote themselves to acquire deeper understanding of religion and thus be able to warn people when they return to them – thus that they (may learn) to guard themselves (against evil).

(al-Tawbah 9: 122)

قَالَ رَسُولُ اللَّهِ صَلَّى اللَّهُ عَلَيْهِ وَسَلَّمَ مَنْ يُرِدْ اللَّهُ بِهِ خَيْرًا
يُفَقِّهْهُ فِي الدِّينِ

(متفق عليه)

The Prophet (peace be upon him) said: "On whomsoever Allah wants to bestow goodness He gives him insight into *Dīn*."

(Bukhārī and Muslim)

As Muslims, we are required to follow the teachings of the Qur'ān and the *Sunnah* in all spheres of our lives. The Holy Qur'ān gives guidance and broad principles as to how we should conduct ourselves. The *Sunnah* records the details of how the Prophet (peace be upon him) implemented this guidance into practice. For example, the Qur'ān has prescribed Prayers for us but it does not give details as to how to pray and precise number of times to pray. The Prophet, however, following the Guidance given by Allah has laid down precise details for us. The same is true for Fasting, *Zakāh* and *Ḥajj* and all other aspects of life such as business transactions, political, legal and social issues.

During the life of the Prophet (peace be upon him) he was the source of all guidance and legislation. After his death, *Khulafā' al-Rāshidūn* – the Rightly-Guided – led the Islamic State and dealt with all new problems in the light of the Qur'ān and the *Sunnah* and tried to reach a consensus – *Ijmā'* – among themselves. The methodology of using one's own reason (*Ijtihād*) to solve new situations enjoyed the approval of the Prophet (peace be upon him). The following conversation between the Prophet (peace be upon him) and Mu'ādh ibn Jabal, when he was appointed Governor of Yemen, illustrates the validity of *Ijtihād*:

عَنْ مُعَاذ أَنَّ رَسُولَ اللَّهِ صَلَّى اللَّهُ عَلَيْهِ وَسَلَّمَ حِينَ بَعَثَهُ إِلَى الْيَمَنِ فَقَالَ كَيْفَ تَصْنَعُ إِنْ عَرَضَ لَكَ قَضَاءٌ قَالَ أَقْضِي بِمَا فِي كِتَابِ اللَّهِ قَالَ فَإِنْ لَمْ يَكُنْ فِي كِتَابِ اللَّهِ قَالَ فَبِسُنَّةِ رَسُولِ اللَّهِ صَلَّى اللَّهُ عَلَيْهِ وَسَلَّمَ قَالَ فَإِنْ لَمْ يَكُنْ فِي سُنَّةِ رَسُولِ اللَّهِ صَلَّى اللَّهُ عَلَيْهِ وَسَلَّمَ قَالَ أَجْتَهِدُ رَأْيِي و لاَ آلُو قَالَ فَضَرَبَ رَسُولُ اللَّهِ صَلَّى اللَّهُ عَلَيْهِ وَسَلَّمَ صَدْرِي ثُمَّ قَالَ الْحَمْدُ لِلَّهِ الَّذِي وَفَّقَ رَسُولَ رَسُولِ اللَّهِ صَلَّى اللَّهُ عَلَيْهِ وَسَلَّمَ لِمَا يُرْضِي رَسُولَ اللَّهِ صَلَّى اللَّهُ عَلَيْهِ وَسَلَّمَ

(الترمذي)

The Prophet (peace be upon him) asked: "What will you do if a matter is referred to you for judgement?" Mu'ādh said: "I will judge according to the Book of Allah." The Prophet asked: "What if you find no explicit guidance in the Book of Allah?" Mu'ādh said: "Then I will judge by the *Sunnah* of the Prophet." The Prophet asked: "And what if you do not find it in the *Sunnah* of the Prophet?" Mu'ādh said: "Then I shall exercise my own judgement and exert to the utmost

(*Ijtihād*) to do the right." The Prophet patted Mu'ādh's chest and said: "Praise be to Allah Who has guided the messenger of His Prophet to that which pleases Him and His Prophet."

(Tirmidhī)

When the institution of *Khilāfah* changed into that of monarchy during the Umayyad period and there was civil war between different factions, the people approached distinguished jurists (*Fuqahā'*) to seek *fatwā* on all issues. Then, with the expansion of the Islamic State from North Africa to Central Asia and the conversion of a multitude of different nationalities into the fold of Islam meant that not many people knew Arabic, nor were they well versed in the sciences of the Qur'ān and *Ḥadīth*. In order to make the practice of Islam easy and accessible to common folk, the *Fuqahā'* codified the *Fiqh* – Islamic law based on the Qur'ān, the *Sunnah*, the *Ijmā'* of the Companions and their own *Ijtihād*. They also developed what is known as *Uṣūl al-Fiqh* (Principles of Jurisprudence), spelling out the methodology through which laws could be derived from the original sources of the Qur'ān and the *Sunnah*.

The literal meaning of *Fiqh* is "to investigate, to search, to open". Imām Ghazālī defines it as understanding and having insight in *Dīn*. This is the meaning in which the word is used in the verse of *Sūrah al-Tawbah* and the *ḥadīth* recited at the beginning of this *Khuṭbah*. Thus, so as to be able to tackle new issues, the *Fuqahā'* exercised *Ijtihād*. The following four schools of *Fiqh* gained wide acceptance by the *Ummah*:

The Ḥanafī School was founded by Imām Abū Ḥanīfah Nu'mān ibn Thābit (80–150 AH/699–767 AC). He was a renowned scholar in Kufa and had, among others, two very eminent jurists, Imām Abū Yūsuf and Imām Muḥammad al-Shaybānī as his disciples. He founded a Council of Scholars including his leading disciples who used to debate all new problems and issues and codified the law. They also recorded whether a *fatwā* was on the basis of a consensus within the group or based on a majority view. Imām Abū Ḥanīfah led and presided over the proceedings. According to reliable estimates, he gave opinions on 83,000 issues dealing with matters relating to civil law, criminal law, evidence, procedures, judicial and international law. Even today, the Ḥanafī School has the largest following. The majority of Muslims in the Indo-Pak subcontinent, Afghanistan, Central Asia and Turkey are Ḥanafī.

The second School of *Fiqh* is Mālikī. Imām Mālik ibn Anas (93–179 AH/711–795 AC) was a contemporary of Imām Abū Ḥanīfah. He was famous for his piety, personal character and scholarship. Spending all his life in Madinah, he devoted himself entirely to learning and teaching. His famous book, *al-Muwaṭṭa'*, is one of the earliest books which forms a link between the *fiqh* literature and the *ḥadīth* collections of later times. *Al-Muwaṭṭa'* contains the *aḥādīth* of the Prophet, the legal opinions of the Companions and the *Tābi'ūn* – successors as well as some later authorities. So immense was the popularity and authority of this book that Khalīfah Abū Ja'far wanted it to be promulgated as the law of the state all over the Islamic world. Imām Mālik disagreed and resisted, his move emphasising that there is more than one choice in practising Islam. The majority of Mālikīs can be found in North Africa, except Egypt, and in West Africa and Arabia.

Imām Muḥammad ibn Idrīs al-Shāfi'ī (150–204 AH/ 767–820 AC), the founder of the third important School of *Fiqh,* was born in Palestine and was a pupil of Imām Mālik. After the death of Imām Mālik he moved to Yemen and then to Baghdad during the reign of Hārūn al-Rashīd. Here, he met Imām Muḥammad, a disciple of Abū Ḥanīfah who acquainted him with the *fiqh* of this School and enlarged his knowledge. From Baghdad he moved to Egypt and there he settled. He is considered to be the chief architect of the principles of Islamic jurisprudence – *Uṣūl al-Fiqh*. His treatises on jurisprudence under the title of *al-Risālah* is a monumental work which indicates his clear vision and full grasp of legal knowledge. Modern scholars consider him one of the greatest jurists of Islam. Followers of the Shāfi'ī School mostly live in Egypt, East Africa, and the West Coast of India and South East Asia.

Imām Aḥmad ibn Ḥanbal (164–241 AH/780–855AC), the last of the great jurists, was born in Baghdad and was a follower of the Shāfi'ī School. He was a man of saintly character and more of a *Muḥaddith* than a jurist. Thus, some authorities do not recognise him as a founder of a new school of *Fiqh*. His outstanding book is *Musnad*, containing more than 40,000 *aḥādīth*, arranged alphabetically by the name of the transmitters. As there is no subject arrangement it is, however, difficult to use. He challenged the Khalīfah al-Ma'mūn and al-Wāthiq and refused to accept the doctrine that the Qur'ān is created. He was imprisoned and persecuted for this. He was later released by Khalīfah al-Mutawakkil, who wanted to bestow favours on him but which he refused. The Ḥanbalīs are mainly to be found in Saudi Arabia.

These are the four *Sunnī* schools of *Fiqh* that have survived to this day. There were other schools, but these did not gain sufficient following. There is though another school of *Fiqh* that does not accept any recognised Imām. They follow the *Sunnah* of the Prophet and are called *Ahl al-Ḥadīth* or *Salafīs*. As they follow the opinions of Imām Ibn Taymiyyah and Imām ʿAbdul Wahhāb, they are sometimes referred to as *Wahhābīs*. Most of the followers of this School live in Saudi Arabia and some in the Indo-Pak subcontinent. Then there is the *Fiqh* of Imām Jaʿfar al-Ṣādiq which is followed by *Shīʿahs* in Iran, Iraq and elsewhere. There are two other Shiʿah schools of *Fiqh,* namely Zaidiyyahs (mainly in Yemen) and Ismāʿīlīs to be found in the Indo-Pak subcontinent and East Africa.

Sometimes people become dismayed and perturbed by these various schools of *Fiqh* and ask why we do not have just one system. First of all, it should be realised that all Schools are unanimous in accepting the Qur'ān and the *Sunnah* as the two fundamental sources of the *Sharīʿah*. Thus, there are no differences in *ʿAqā'id* (beliefs) and *Muʿāmalāt* (social dealings). There is agreement in the central core of *ʿIbādah* – only in details there are some differences. On the whole, on almost 90 percent of legal matters there is unanimity. Only some 10 percent is subject to differences, mostly in minor details. These differences are either due to a different interpretation of a Qur'ānic text or *aḥādīth* or due to the fact that the Prophet at different times performed certain acts in different ways. The other reason for such differences is due to their *Ijtihād*, when there is no guidance available in the Qur'ān and the *Sunnah*. Those Companions who saw him perform *Ṣalāh* in one way followed that while others observed him in a slightly different way and followed that. Thus, whichever way one follows it is in obedience to the Prophet (peace be upon him). The differences point to what were preferred by one school for genuine reasons. These differences in a way showed the degree of flexibility within the system. As human beings each of us has a different way of thinking. As long as this is based on the Qur'ān and the *Sunnah* whatever conclusion the *fuqahā'* arrived at deserves to be respected. One has every right to follow what one thinks preferable. Differences should be tolerated.

Some people become very rigid in their attitude and regard all other Schools except their own as invalid. This rigidity and extremism has caused some friction between Muslims in different parts of the world, including Britain. Sometimes this has even led to bloodshed and violence. But we should remember that if Allah wanted us to have one uniform system His Prophet would not have varied the ways in his actions. Finally, this diversity is a consequence of human ingenuity in solving problems. This provides variety and colour in life otherwise there would be nothing but drab uniformity.

Our *fuqahā'* have accepted these differences and respected the views of others despite their disagreements with them. I have already mentioned the view of Imām Mālik that he was opposed to the imposition of his *fiqh* as the sole Code of Law in the Islamic State. It is also recorded that when Imām Shāfi'ī visited the Mosque of Imām Abū Ḥanīfah, he followed the way in which the Ḥanafīs pray. When he was asked why he did this, he said that he did so out of respect for the one buried nearby. Thus, we see how liberal and tolerant our Imāms were towards different points of view. They accepted the rights of others to have their own opinions while still disagreeing with them. Yet their followers who have far less knowledge fight each other on insignificant matters!

Thus, we should have the magnanimity to accept the views of others and the *Fiqh* they follow. There are far more important things on which we agree. These minor details on which the Law-Giver has allowed variation should be tolerated by us all. Let us pray that Allah (*swt*) gives us true understanding of His *Dīn* and makes us magnanimous and tolerant in attitude so that we respect each other's points of view and do not try to impose our views on others. (*Āmīn*).

The *Sīrah* of the Prophet

وَإِنَّكَ لَعَلَىٰ خُلُقٍ عَظِيمٍ ﴿٤﴾

And you (stand) on an exalted standard of character.
(al-Qalam 68: 4)

وَمَآ أَرْسَلْنَٰكَ إِلَّا رَحْمَةً لِّلْعَٰلَمِينَ ﴿١٠٧﴾

We have not sent you, but as a mercy for all beings.
(al-Anbiyā' 21: 107)

Our Prophet (peace be upon him) is a gift of mercy to humanity. He was sent for the purpose of perfecting good morals. It is narrated by Imām Mālik that the Prophet (peace be upon him) said:

إِنَّما بُعِثْتُ لِأُتَمِّمَ مَكَارِمَ الأَخْلَاقِ

(ألموطّأ)

"I have been sent to complete the best moral standards."
(al-Muwaṭṭa')

So what were his morals? Some people came to *Umm al-Mu'minīn* 'Ā'ishah and asked her to describe the morals of the Prophet. She said:

كَانَ خُلُقُهُ الْقُرْآنَ

(متفق عليه)

"His morals were the embodiment of the Qur'ān."
(Bukhārī and Muslim)

Thus he was the living and personified embodiment of the Qur'ān on earth. Allah (*swt*) testifies to this fact when He says: O Muḥammad! You stand on the exalted standard of character.

Usually we see people propound high moral values and establish grand principles but often their own practices fall short of these standards. It is the perfect life of the Prophet that shows that he lived up to all the principles he preached. He meticulously followed all the injunctions revealed to him and he practised all Qur'ānic teachings in his private and public life.

When we talk about morality we usually restrict it to a few moral attributes such as kindness, generosity and humbleness. But moral values embrace the whole gamut of life. These are manifested in our dealings in all situations: whether it is with friends or foes; in prosperity or adversity; in peace or in war; in public or in private. Thus, if we were to study the *Sīrah* of the Prophet comprehensively we would observe that he occupies the highest pedestal of morality.

The testimony of those who are close to a person is more valuable than of those who come into contact with someone infrequently. A person could pretend to be good mannered in public but in his private life reveal his true nature. He may display his best behaviour in public but be unable to hide his true nature from those with whom he has intimate relations. Who can be in closer contact with a husband than his wife? She shares the secrets of his life and knows his character much better than anyone else.

Look at the testimony of the Prophet's wife *Umm al-Mu'minīn* Khadījah when he returned home after receiving his call to Prophethood. He was trembling and asked her to cover him. She comforted him, saying:

كَلاَّ وَاللَّهِ مَا يُخْزِيكَ اللَّهُ أَبَدًا إِنَّكَ لَتَصِلُ الرَّحِمَ وَتَحْمِلُ الْكَلَّ
وَتَكْسِبُ الْمَعْدُومَ وَتَقْرِي الضَّيْفَ وَتُعِينُ عَلَى نَوَائِبِ الْحَقِّ

(البخاري)

"No, you have nothing to fear. God will never let you down, you are kind to your relatives, you are astute and patient, you give to the needy, you are generous to guests and you never fail to relieve people from distress."

(Bukhārī)

We have already seen what *Umm al-Mu'minīn* 'Ā'ishah said about his character in so far as his life was the manifestation of the Qur'ān. She also narrated extensively about his character and qualities. She said: "He did not scold anyone, nor did he take revenge on anyone. He used to forgive and pardon those who oppressed him. He never abused anyone. He never hit anyone, not even an animal. He never refused any request unless of course it were illegal. Whenever he used to come home he was always cheerful and smiling."

'Alī ibn Abī Ṭālib, his cousin, who was one of first young persons to accept Islam and lived with the Prophet for 23 years, testified to the very high standard of his character. Once, his son Ḥusain asked him about the Prophet's character and habits. He said: "The Prophet was of smiling countenance, gentle and generous. He was neither bad tempered nor narrow-minded. He never agitated over frivolous things. He never uttered a bad word nor did he find fault with others. If he disliked anything he would ignore it but he did not show his approval either. People who knew his disposition realised from his facial expressions what his intentions were. He refrained from controversial debates, unnecessary talking and unrelated issues."

One important aspect of moral behaviour is constancy. One should be firm and persevere along the path one has chosen. One should not be capricious and follow one's whims. This is very evident from the life of the Prophet. Once he established a practice, he followed it strictly. The word *Sunnah* in the *Sharī'ah* conveys this meaning. These were the acts the Prophet constantly observed. The Prophet (peace be upon him) used to say:

إِنَّ أَحَبَّ الأَعْمَالِ إِلَى اللَّهِ أَدْوَمُهَا وَإِنْ قَلَّ

(البخاري)

"The most loved act to God is the one that is performed regularly even it was a little."

(Bukhārī)

He was always fair in his dealings with others. Even before his Prophethood, when he was involved in commercial dealings people always trusted him. He was known by the title of *al-Amīn* – the Trustworthy. Though the Quraysh rejected his message they never questioned his honesty. Even before his migration to Madinah he held trust money from various people and he left these with 'Alī to return them to their owners.

The most prominent feature of his character was his selflessness. There are many instances that show how he sacrificed his own needs for the sake of others. Once a woman presented him with a shawl that he needed. One of his Companions came and praised it. He gave it to him. When the Prophet left the gathering, others rebuked that person saying you knew how badly the Prophet needed this shawl. And he would never reject any request. The person replied: "Yes, but I took it for *barakah*, I wanted it to be used as my shroud."

He was indeed a very humble person. He used to do all his household chores himself. He repaired his own clothes, cleaned his house, did his own shopping and even mended his own shoes. He used to mingle with the poor and the slaves and would even eat with them. He stopped people standing up and greeting him like a noble man. He used to sit wherever there was a place available in an assembly and never sought a prominent or elevated position. Thus, a newcomer would not know that he was the Prophet. Usually, a person becomes proud and haughty when he acquires power and when thousands of people follow him and are ready to sacrifice their lives for him. Yet when the Prophet entered Makkah as a conqueror with a huge army we see him prostrating in humility and his forehead touching the saddle of his camel.

Above all other qualities that he possessed, the quality of his mercy was the most prominent. Allah (*swt*) says: "We have not sent you, but as a mercy to all beings." There are very many instances in his *Sīrah* that illustrate his profound mercy for everyone, whether friend or enemy, Muslim or non-Muslim, young or old, human or animal. Once when someone asked him to curse an enemy he became angry and said that he had not come to this world to curse people; rather I am sent as a mercy. He used to advise his Companions:

لاَ تَحَاسَدُوا وَلاَ تَنَاجَشُوا وَلاَ تَبَاغَضُوا وَلاَ تَدَابَرُوا
وَكُونُوا عِبَادَ اللَّهِ إِخْوَانًا

(مسلم)

"Do not hate each other, and do not envy each other and do not abandon each other. You are Allah's servants so be like brothers."

(Muslim)

He commanded:

لاَ يُؤْمِنُ أَحَدُكُمْ حَتَّى يُحِبَّ لأَخِيهِ مَا يُحِبُّ لِنَفْسِهِ

(احمد)

"None of you could be a perfect *Mu'min* unless you like for others what you like for yourselves."

(Aḥmad)

The Quraysh, who persecuted him in Makkah and fought several battles against him, were pardoned by him after the conquest of Makkah. Even in Taif, where he was beaten up, ridiculed and driven out of town by people, this still did not attract any curse from him. Rather he said, maybe their descendants will accept Islam. 'Ikramah, the son of his arch enemy Abū Jahl escaped after the conquest of Makkah, and when he came to Madinah he greeted and pardoned him. As for 'Abdullāh ibn Ubayy who was a hypocrite through and through and who always conspired against Muslims,he was granted the Prophet's shirt for his shroud and the Prophet even led his funeral Prayer and prayed for his *maghfirah.* When 'Umar objected, saying: "O Prophet of Allah! You are leading his funeral Prayer and he said this and this." The Prophet smiled and said: "If I have been given the choice I will pray even seventy times or more if I know he can be pardoned (by Allah)."

Such was the character and high moral standard of our Prophet. This is the reason that Allah (*swt*) advised us:

لَّقَدْ كَانَ لَكُمْ فِي رَسُولِ ٱللَّهِ أُسْوَةٌ حَسَنَةٌ … ﴿٢١﴾

You have indeed in the Messenger of Allah a beautiful pattern of conduct.

(al-Aḥzāb 33: 21)

His life, sufferings and triumphs will remain for Muslims and non-Muslims alike a symbol of modesty, faithful devotion, service to God, a life example for us all to follow. He was a kind, merciful and compassionate person who did not abuse anyone and freely pardoned his enemies. He lived a simple and modest life. Submission to the will of God and service to humanity are the essence of his teachings.

Let us pray that Allah may bless the Prophet, his family and his Companions. May Allah elevate him to *Maqām al-Maḥmūd* in Heaven. Let us earnestly try and follow his exemplary life and devote ourselves to the same struggle of witnessing the truth to the whole of mankind. (*Āmīn.*)

Morality

لَّيْسَ ٱلْبِرَّ أَن تُوَلُّوا۟ وُجُوهَكُمْ قِبَلَ ٱلْمَشْرِقِ وَٱلْمَغْرِبِ وَلَـٰكِنَّ ٱلْبِرَّ
مَنْ ءَامَنَ بِٱللَّهِ وَٱلْيَوْمِ ٱلْـَٔاخِرِ وَٱلْمَلَـٰٓئِكَةِ وَٱلْكِتَـٰبِ وَٱلنَّبِيِّـۧنَ وَءَاتَى
ٱلْمَالَ عَلَىٰ حُبِّهِۦ ذَوِى ٱلْقُرْبَىٰ وَٱلْيَتَـٰمَىٰ وَٱلْمَسَـٰكِينَ وَٱبْنَ ٱلسَّبِيلِ
وَٱلسَّآئِلِينَ وَفِى ٱلرِّقَابِ وَأَقَامَ ٱلصَّلَوٰةَ وَءَاتَى ٱلزَّكَوٰةَ وَٱلْمُوفُونَ
بِعَهْدِهِمْ إِذَا عَـٰهَدُوا۟ ۖ وَٱلصَّـٰبِرِينَ فِى ٱلْبَأْسَآءِ وَٱلضَّرَّآءِ وَحِينَ ٱلْبَأْسِ ۗ
أُو۟لَـٰٓئِكَ ٱلَّذِينَ صَدَقُوا۟ ۖ وَأُو۟لَـٰٓئِكَ هُمُ ٱلْمُتَّقُونَ ﴿١٧٧﴾

It is not righteousness that you turn your faces towards East or West. But it is righteousness to believe in Allah and the Last Day and the Angels and the Book and the Messengers; to spend of your substance out of love of Him, for your relations, for orphans, for the needy, for the wayfarers, for those who beg and for the ransom of slaves; to be steadfast in Prayer and practise regular charity, to fulfil the obligations which you have made and to be firm and patient in pain (or suffering) and adversity and throughout all periods of panic. Such are the people of truth and God-fearing.

(al-Baqarah 2: 177)

We live in a law-abiding universe. There are the laws of gravity, laws of physics, of chemistry, of motion and of thermodynamics. We did not make these laws, but over the centuries we have learned to define and respect them. We study the laws that govern our universe. We design our aircraft and spacecraft so they can fly observing those laws. We predict the motions of the planets and stars so that we can send our rockets precisely following the laws of nature. It would be arrogant and foolish if we ignored these laws or tried to conflict with them.

So what makes us think that we can disregard laws governing morality? It is the moral law which shows us the difference between what is right and what is wrong. Every society has recognised that it must have laws to live by. When laws are kept, society is stable and prospers. When laws are broken, the offenders are pursued and penalties imposed so that society can live in peace and harmony. There is a consensus of public opinion that the laws are to be obeyed and offenders punished. But if enough people break the laws for long enough, the consensus dissolves and society is challenged and law and order crumbles. Then there is chaos and disorder.

It is not only the advanced societies that follow a moral code of law. Even primitive societies like the Pygmies of Central Africa have a body of moral law and practice and they do not deviate from it. There is an inborn sense of morality in all human beings. Throughout the ages there have been certain qualities that have been warmly approved of by society, while others have been consistently condemned. We all appreciate truthfulness, charity, courage, honesty, hospitality, loyalty, sympathy, fidelity, justice and many other good qualities. Equally, we disdain hypocrisy, bigotry, injustice, falsehood, betrayal, infidelity, cowardice, cruelty and rudeness. When they become part of the collective behaviour of society, these personal moral values bring about a just, compassionate and morally upright society and state.

If the distinction between good and evil is universal and clear-cut then why is there so much muddled thinking and confusion in public life? If we reflect on these issues we find that moral laws cannot be enforced in a vacuum. They cannot be upheld without sanctions. Ethical philosophy and the code of moral behaviour for individuals and society is based on the concept of the universe, man's place in it and man's purpose on earth and whether he is accountable for his actions to his Creator. These are fundamental questions that have to be settled first.

It is the mercy of Allah (*swt*) that He has given us the basic instincts to differentiate between good and evil. But human affairs are much more complex and need more precise guidance. Thus, Allah (*swt*), who has provided for the fulfilment of our physical needs on this earth, has also provided detailed guidance through His Prophets – Ādam, Ibrāhīm, Mūsā, ʿĪsā and Muḥammad (peace be upon them all). He gave them Scriptures that laid down the law like the Ten Commandments. It is God who made these laws just like He made physical laws to govern the universe.

Islam is based on the guidance received from Allah. It ensures that the whole edifice of society is built on moral values and sets out to generate good and suppress evil. Personal moral values are encouraged and upheld by the wholesome environment of society. Thus, morality and piety prosper and evil forces are rigorously controlled.

Islam is a natural way of life. It is a balanced system of life. Allah, the Creator, knows human virtues as well as weaknesses. Thus, Islam does not lay so heavy a burden on mankind that human beings cannot carry it out. Islam recognises the legitimate needs of human beings and makes provision for their fulfilment.

Today, people question the Guidance given by God. They deny that Allah has sent Revelations to His Messengers to provide guidance for mankind. People think they are mature enough to lay down their own laws. There are several powerful ideas that have dominated our thinking. The three that have revolutionised the scientific thought of modern times are Charles Darwin, Karl Marx and Sigmund Freud. They transformed scientific thinking in biology, economics, philosophy and psychology.

Darwin published his *The Origin of Species,* in 1859, which challenged the Biblical narration of the creation of the universe. One of the concepts on which his theory of evolution was based supposed the survival of the fittest and this paved the way for colonial powers to exploit the helpless peoples of Asia and Africa. It brought human beings to the level of animals with no values and no morality.

Karl Marx published his *Das Kapital* and the *Communist Manifesto* during the middle of the 19th century. They paved the way for the totalitarian communist regimes of the former Soviet Union, Eastern Europe and other parts of the world. Based on atheism, these societies dispensed with all Divine guidance. They proclaimed that man is only motivated by economic necessities. All history is the history of class war.

Similarly, Freud with his theory of the human mind proclaimed the sexual urge is the most powerful force in human motivation. All three of them looked at the baser instincts of man and ignored the moral code of laws that govern human societies. Thus, we have chaos everywhere. We kill thousands of embryos – potential human beings – and perform abortions to kill unborn babies. There is uncontrolled sexual anarchy. Our youth are addicted to drugs. Pornography and the shameful exploitation of women is rife. Where is our moral sense? We are violating the laws of Nature. We are demeaning the guidance of God.

We, as Muslims, who claim that we have guidance from Allah, are neglectful of our duty. The knowledge and guidance that we possess demands responsibility which in turn creates accountability. We have a duty to inform our society that it is breaking the laws of God. Times change, but the laws of God do not change. The penalty for breaking the laws will be the same as they were thousands of years ago. The people of Lūṭ broke the laws of morality, the people of Shuʿayb broke the laws of fair dealing in trade, Banī Isrā'īl rejected the tenets of the *Tawrāt*. You know how Allah dealt with each of these transgressors. If Muslims living in this society do not try to change the situation and do not protest and inform others about their crimes, they are equally guilty and cannot escape punishment from Allah. As Allah says:

وَلَن تَجِدَ لِسُنَّةِ ٱللَّهِ تَبۡدِيلٗا ٦٢

No change will you find in the practice (approved) of Allah.
(al-Aḥzāb 33: 62)

I hope and pray that we realise our duty and inform our society about Islamic teachings on morality. As you know, moral values are given by Almighty Allah to all people from time immemorial and they have continued to be upheld by successive generations. Islam has preserved them intact for the whole of humanity to practise so that they remain the guiding principles forever.

May Allah guide us all to honour His Commandments and have them prevail throughout our society. (*Āmīn.*)

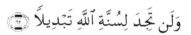

Tazkiyah

هُوَ ٱلَّذِى بَعَثَ فِى ٱلْأُمِّيِّـۧنَ رَسُولًا مِّنْهُمْ يَتْلُوا۟ عَلَيْهِمْ ءَايَـٰتِهِۦ وَيُزَكِّيهِمْ
وَيُعَلِّمُهُمُ ٱلْكِتَـٰبَ وَٱلْحِكْمَةَ وَإِن كَانُوا۟ مِن قَبْلُ لَفِى ضَلَـٰلٍ مُّبِينٍ ﴿٢﴾

It is He Who has sent among the Unlettered a Messenger from among themselves, to rehearse to them His Signs, to purify them, and to instruct them in Scripture and Wisdom – although they had been, before, in manifest error.

(al-Jumuʿah 62: 2)

It is only human nature to desire improvement, to make progress, to succeed in life and to achieve goals. Even others, for example members of our family and our friends, expect us to excel, to win and to be successful in our endeavours.

Those of you who are studying a Business Management course know the emphasis placed on self-development to improve the performance of an individual and of a company. Management experts recognise that the human resource is the most valuable asset. No social organisation can achieve success unless it has human resources available to lead it. Thus mundane bodies like a business organisation require more than any other resource the best human capital.

Islam, which aims for the transformation of human society and fashions it according to its revolutionary ideology, cannot achieve its objectives without valuable and dependable human resources.

We observe that human beings come in all shapes and sizes. Each one of us is unique. Even our fingerprints are different. Current research in genetics has discovered that each person's DNA structure is different.

The genetic code of each of us is unique. There are so many variations in human beings. We not only differ in physical detail but also in our psychology, behavioural patterns and attitudes. It is not possible to mould us into the same shape and size. Actually, there is no need to destroy the richness and variety that the Creator has intended to be preserved.

What Islam requires is that human beings be trained to behave in a predictable way within certain limits. Thus, if they are asked to assemble for Prayers at a certain time, the majority of them will turn up. If they are asked to give their wealth most will provide their money. If they are asked to sacrifice their lives, the majority, if not all, will be ready for this.

In Qur'ānic terminology, the word used for this training or what we call in modern management terminology self-development, is *Tazkiyah* which also includes spiritual development. As human beings need both physical and spiritual development, one of the main functions of the Prophets was to perform this important task of *Tazkiyah*. It encompasses two meanings. One is to cleanse and purify oneself and the other is to grow and improve oneself. Both aspects are complementary. Whatever is clean and pure will certainly prosper according to its potentialities. Thus, the Holy Qur'ān says:

قَدْ أَفْلَحَ مَن تَزَكَّىٰ ﴿١٤﴾

Prosperous is he who has cleansed himself.
(al-A'lā 87: 14)

قَدْ أَفْلَحَ مَن زَكَّىٰهَا ﴿٩﴾ وَقَدْ خَابَ مَن دَسَّىٰهَا ﴿١٠﴾

Truly he succeeds that purifies it; and he fails that corrupts it.
(al-Shams 91: 9–10)

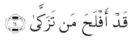

We should understand that the process of spiritual and self-development or *Tazkiyah* cannot be imposed on human beings. It has to be the personal responsibility of each individual. No one can do the job for us. No amount of training or education can train or educate us if we are not willing to be trained or educated. Universities and other organisations can provide all the facilities for our development, but it is the primary duty of the individual to use these facilities to his own advantage.

Thus, the first requirement for *Tazkiyah* is our commitment to purify ourselves. Once we assume this responsibility there should be a firm determination and commitment to remain steadfast and not to quiver. A word of caution here – determination should not be confused with wishful thinking. A mere wishing will not achieve anything. As the saying goes – if wishes were horses, beggars would ride. Once a firm commitment is made there should not be doubt or hesitation.

Next is our ceaseless effort to improve ourselves. Once determination is made to achieve the desired results then we should embark upon the path of hard struggle. No half-hearted effort will bear fruit. We should realise that these efforts and struggles are lifelong commitments that we have to undertake. There are no shortcuts. But once we are on the way there is unlimited potential for growth.

The third requirement is sincerity in our efforts. Of course, unless there is grace from Allah and His *Tawfīq* we cannot achieve anything. But this is given only to those who are *Mu'min* and those who are sincere in their Faith. Thus, we have to seek His *Isti'ānah* (help). Without Allah's help and aid we cannot traverse this path. We will face trials and tribulations. These tests are of course necessary for our purification. They are there to distinguish between those who are sincere and those who are hypocrites. Thus, constant prayers and seeking Allah's guidance and help is essential.

All these steps are beautifully summed up in the *āyah* from *Sūrah Banī Isrā'īl*:

وَمَنْ أَرَادَ ٱلْءَاخِرَةَ وَسَعَىٰ لَهَا سَعْيَهَا وَهُوَ مُؤْمِنٌ فَأُو۟لَٰٓئِكَ

كَانَ سَعْيُهُم مَّشْكُورًا ١٩

And whosoever desires the Hereafter and strives after it with the effort necessary, being a believer, they are the ones whose striving is acceptable to Allah.

(Banī Isrā'īl 17: 19)

I have outlined the important requirements for achieving self-purification. But with any programme of action there needs to be a model to facilitate its implementation. Thus, we need a perfect model before us so that we can attempt to model our lives accordingly. Allah (*swt*) has provided the *Sīrah* of the Prophet (peace be upon him) a perfect model for us:

لَّقَدْ كَانَ لَكُمْ فِى رَسُولِ ٱللَّهِ أُسْوَةٌ حَسَنَةٌ لِّمَن كَانَ يَرْجُوا۟ ٱللَّهَ
وَٱلْيَوْمَ ٱلْءَاخِرَ وَذَكَرَ ٱللَّهَ كَثِيرًا ﴿٢١﴾

You have indeed in the Messenger of Allah a beautiful pattern (of conduct) for any one whose hope is in Allah and the Final Day, and who engages much in the praise of Allah.
(al-Aḥzāb 33: 21)

The study of *Sīrah* teaches us that *Tazkiyah* should be comprehensive and balanced. The most important aspect of the Prophet's life was his moderation and well-balanced conduct. He stopped his Companions from praying all night, or fasting continuously or living a life of celibacy. He said that I excel you in piety but I pray at night and sleep as well; I fast and abstain from fasting and I live a married life.

We know that in Islam all acts of *'Ibādah* are communal. Thus brotherhood and community life is essential for achieving self-purification. It is vital for us to develop a strong bond of brotherhood to sustain the seed of *Īmān*. Brotherhood reinforces human potentiality and commitment. Thus, the Holy Qur'ān instructs the Prophet (peace be upon him):

وَٱصْبِرْ نَفْسَكَ مَعَ ٱلَّذِينَ يَدْعُونَ رَبَّهُم بِٱلْغَدَوٰةِ وَٱلْعَشِىِّ ... ﴿٢٨﴾

You bind yourself with those who call upon Allah morning and evening.
(al-Kahf 18: 28)

An eminent scholar of the Indo-Pak subcontinent, Shaikh 'Uthmān ibn 'Alī al-Hujwirī in his famous book *Kashf al-Maḥjūb* related a story that a person who was performing *Ṭawāf* in the Ka'bah was praying: "O Lord! Make my friends pious." He was asked why at this blessed place you are not praying for yourself but only for your friends? He replied: "I will return to my friends from here, if they are pious I will become pious in their company. If they are evil I will be the same with them."

Modern psychological research also confirms that peer influence is a very powerful agent in human behaviour. Group life is the most powerful force to stimulate and inspire people. Thus, it is essential that we keep the company of those who are our fellow travellers.

It is natural that the way we found beneficial for our self-development and purification should lead us to strive and to invite others to the path of Allah. This will increase our own commitment. It stimulates the *Īmān* and enhances our steadfastness. With the support of a group of brothers, each reinforcing the other, the whole of life becomes integrated and this makes it easy for us to traverse the path of righteousness and truth:

وَمَنْ أَحْسَنُ قَوْلًا مِّمَّن دَعَآ إِلَى ٱللَّهِ وَعَمِلَ صَٰلِحًا
وَقَالَ إِنَّنِى مِنَ ٱلْمُسْلِمِينَ ﴿٣٣﴾

Who is better in speech than one who invites (people) to Allah, works righteousness and says, "I am of those who bow in Islam"?
(Fuṣṣilat 41: 33)

Let us pray that Allah (*swt*) give us *Tawfīq* to embark upon the path of *Tazkiyah,* to make a firm determination and ceaseless effort so that we can achieve self-purification for ourselves and our friends and relations. (*Āmīn.*)

Tazkiyah: Practical Steps

لَقَدْ مَنَّ ٱللَّهُ عَلَى ٱلْمُؤْمِنِينَ إِذْ بَعَثَ فِيهِمْ رَسُولًا مِّنْ أَنفُسِهِمْ يَتْلُوا۟
عَلَيْهِمْ ءَايَـٰتِهِۦ وَيُزَكِّيهِمْ وَيُعَلِّمُهُمُ ٱلْكِتَـٰبَ وَٱلْحِكْمَةَ وَإِن
كَانُوا۟ مِن قَبْلُ لَفِى ضَلَـٰلٍ مُّبِينٍ ﴿١٦٤﴾

Allah did confer a great favour on the Believers when He sent among them a Messenger from among themselves, rehearsing unto them the Signs of Allah, purifying them. And instructing them in Scripture and Wisdom, while before that, they had been in manifest error.

(Āl ʿImrān 3: 164)

One of the main functions which Prophets performed was *Tazkiyah*. It was the duty of the Prophets to lead the way and guide people to a life of piety. As we have discussed in a previous *Khuṭbah*, it is the responsibility of the individual to take charge of his spiritual and self-development. Each and every one of us should have the commitment to improve oneself. We should struggle and make efforts to achieve this. But this can only be done with sincerity and with the help of Allah. The model before us is the life of the Prophet (peace be upon him).

Having said this, each one of us has to work within the broad framework provided to us by our *Dīn*. The question is from where do we start this work of *Tazkiyah*?

The place to start is with what in Qur'ānic terminology is called *Qalb* (heart). By this I do not mean the piece of flesh which pumps blood through the body. But it is the inner self, the faculty of reason, the soul, whatever motivates a person to do something. It is the source of human reason and emotion. It is the centre of one's personality. It is the place where *Īmān* and conviction reside. It is also the place that is afflicted by disease:

فِي قُلُوبِهِم مَّرَضٌ ... ﴿١٠﴾

In their hearts is a disease...

(al-Baqarah 2: 10)

It is also where doubts and hypocrisy reside:

قَالَتِ ٱلْأَعْرَابُ ءَامَنَّا ۖ قُل لَّمْ تُؤْمِنُوا۟ وَلَـٰكِن قُولُوٓا۟ أَسْلَمْنَا
وَلَمَّا يَدْخُلِ ٱلْإِيمَـٰنُ فِى قُلُوبِكُمْ ۖ ... ﴿١٤﴾

The desert Arabs say: "We believe." Say: "You have no faith; but you should say: 'We have submitted our wills to Allah', for not yet has Faith entered your hearts."

(al-Ḥujurāt 49: 14)

The Holy Qur'ān declares no one will be successful,

إِلَّا مَنْ أَتَى ٱللَّهَ بِقَلْبٍ سَلِيمٍ ﴿٨٩﴾

Except the one who comes to Allah with a sound heart.

(al-Shu'arā' 26: 89)

The Prophet (peace be upon him) said:

قَدْ أَفْلَحَ مَنْ أَخْلَصَ قَلْبَهُ لِلْإِيمَانِ وَجَعَلَ قَلْبَهُ سَلِيمًا

(احمد)

He has succeeded whose heart Allah has purified for *Īmān* and made his heart righteous and submissive.

(Aḥmad and Baihaqī *fi Shu'ab al-Īmān*)

Then, the Holy Qur'ān explains the reason behind this:

فَإِنَّهَا لَا تَعْمَى ٱلْأَبْصَـٰرُ وَلَـٰكِن تَعْمَى ٱلْقُلُوبُ ٱلَّتِى فِى ٱلصُّدُورِ ﴿٤٦﴾

It is not the eyes that go blind but it is the heart inside you that goes blind.

(al-Ḥajj 22: 46)

رَسُولَ اللَّهِ صَلَّى اللَّهُ عَلَيْهِ وَسَلَّمَ يَقُولُ أَلاَ وَإِنَّ فِي الْجَسَدِ مُضْغَةً
إِذَا صَلَحَتْ صَلَحَ الْجَسَدُ كُلُّهُ وَإِذَا فَسَدَتْ فَسَدَ الْجَسَدُ
كُلُّهُ أَلاَ وَهِيَ الْقَلْبُ

(متفق عليه)

The Prophet (peace be upon him) said: Truly in the body there is a piece of flesh: if it is healthy, the whole body is healthy and if it is corrupt the whole body is corrupted. Truly it is the heart.

(Bukhārī and Muslim)

This does not mean actions are not important. Even words are important as they have an impact on others. If someone abuses you, naturally you will become angry. By doing wrong actions and by committing sins the heart becomes hardened. Thus, to keep the heart pure you should safeguard the channels which convey messages to the heart. The Prophet (peace be upon him) in the *ḥadīth* quoted above continues as:

الأُذُنُ فَقَمِعٌ وَالْعَيْنُ بِمُقِرَّةٍ لِمَا يُوعَى الْقَلْبُ

(احمد)

Ears are the filters and eyes are the conveyors of images that reach the heart.

(Aḥmad)

Thus, it is essential we safeguard our eyes and ears from pornography, pop music and obscene literature. We should try and seek Allah's help to protect us from these evils. We should follow the example of the Prophet (peace be upon him) who used to pray:

يَا مُقَلِّبَ الْقُلُوبِ ثَبِّتْ قَلْبِي عَلَى دِينِكَ

(احمد)

O Lord! Who changes the hearts, keep my heart firm on Your *Dīn*.

(Aḥmad)

On the Day of Judgement, we will be asked about our faculties. How have we used them? The Qur'ān says:

إِنَّ ٱلسَّمْعَ وَٱلْبَصَرَ وَٱلْفُؤَادَ كُلُّ أُوْلَـٰٓئِكَ كَانَ عَنْهُ مَسْـُٔولًا ﴿٣٦﴾

For every act of hearing or of seeing or of (feeling in) the heart, will be enquired into (on the Day of Reckoning).

(Banī Isrā'īl 17: 36)

How should we safeguard our hearts? How should we keep ourselves within the limits laid down by the *Sharī'ah*? How can we remain on the Straight Path when there are so many temptations? We have so many pre-occupations, there are so many distractions. These are very important and difficult questions. Allah (*swt*) has provided us with the means to overcome these difficulties.

Central to the heart is *Dhikr* (Remembrance). Human beings cannot perform anything without memory. We should always try to remind ourselves of the presence of Allah. This will help us to avoid committing sins. Moreover there are grave consequences in forgetting Allah. When we forget Allah, Allah also forgets us. Thus, we are deprived of His mercy and His blessings. Second, when we forget Allah we also forget ourselves. We do not know what the purpose of our life is. We forget and involve ourselves in this world and become worse than animals.

If we remember Allah, Allah remembers us. Thus, we benefit from His mercy and blessings. It is related that Thābit Banānī, a learned person, said: "I know when my Lord remembers me." People became frightened and asked him: "How do you know that?" He said: "When I remember Him, He remembers me." Then he recited this *āyah*:

فَٱذْكُرُونِىٓ أَذْكُرْكُمْ وَٱشْكُرُوا۟ لِى وَلَا تَكْفُرُونِ ﴿١٥٢﴾

Then you do remember Me; I will remember you. Be grateful to Me, and reject not Faith.

(al-Baqarah 2: 152)

When *Dhikr* is mentioned, the imagery of someone rolling his fingers on *Tasbīḥ* comes to mind. But according to the Qur'ān, our whole life should be *Dhikr*. This *Dhikr* should be with *Fikr* (reflection) as the *āyah* of the Qur'ān expounds:

ٱلَّذِينَ يَذْكُرُونَ ٱللَّهَ قِيَـٰمًا وَقُعُودًا وَعَلَىٰ جُنُوبِهِمْ وَيَتَفَكَّرُونَ فِى خَلْقِ ٱلسَّمَـٰوَٰتِ وَٱلْأَرْضِ ... ﴿١٩١﴾

People who remember Allah, standing, sitting, and lying down on their sides and contemplate the creation in the heavens and the earth.

(Āl 'Imrān 3: 191)

Of course the best form of *Dhikr* is *Ṣalāh* (Prayer). As the purpose of Prayer is to remember Allah, the Holy Qur'ān says:

وَأَقِمِ ٱلصَّلَوٰةَ لِذِكْرِىٓ ﴿١٤﴾

And establish Ṣalāh *for My remembrance.*

(Ṭā Hā 20: 14)

Thus, *Dhikr* should be integrated within our everyday activity.

Remembrance of *Ākhirah* is also part of the *Dhikr* of Allah. Our *Dhikr* is only fruitful when we assimilate it with our concern about our accountability in the *Ākhirah*, when we realise that this life and all its pleasures and bounties are transitory. Whatever is created will be annihilated in the end. All of us have to face death. We do not know when it will come. But death is the most sure thing. Hence it is called *Yaqīn* (certainty). We will be accountable for all our deeds. Nothing will be hidden on that day. Unlike this life, the life in the Hereafter is eternal. The best way to remember *Ākhirah* is to remember death which we see every day around us.

The Prophet (peace be upon him) has beautifully summarised this in his saying that "I am leaving behind two guides for you. One that talks and the other that is silent. The one that talks is the Qur'ān and the one that is silent is Death."

If we pay attention to these two vital guides – the *Dhikr* of Allah and the *Fikr* of *Ākhirah*, then we will be able to live our lives according to the *Sharī'ah*. Still there are weaknesses in our lives that may cloud our vision.

To cure them, Islam has prescribed for us *'Ibādah* – a regular training programme for our spiritual and self-development. If we remain steadfast on our *'Ibādah* then, *Inshā' Allāh*, we will be able to overcome all our weaknesses.

We all know that forgetfulness is our basic weakness and the *Dhikr* and *Ṣalāh* are the reminders to cure this weakness. Love of this worldly life and its glitter sways us from the Path of Righteousness. The remedy for this is *Infāq fī Sabīl Allāh* that removes the love of wealth. Love of carnal self, of eating and drinking and sexual gratification (*Shahwah*) play havoc in our lives and try to lead us astray. Its remedy is *Ṣawm* (fasting) which teaches us self-control. The total remedy for all the diseases of our heart and mind are cured by *Ḥajj*. During *Ḥajj* we are removed from our home and familiar surroundings. We undertake this spiritual and emotional journey to strengthen our *Īmān* and to remind us of our ultimate accountability before Allah (*swt*) on the Day of Judgement.

Let us pray that Allah may lead us away from the temptations of this world and lead us to the path of *Tazkiyah* and *Taqwā* so that we may achieve felicity in *Ākhirah*. (*Āmīn.*)

Dhikr

ٱلَّذِينَ ءَامَنُوا۟ وَتَطْمَئِنُّ قُلُوبُهُم بِذِكْرِ ٱللَّهِ ۗ أَلَا بِذِكْرِ ٱللَّهِ
تَطْمَئِنُّ ٱلْقُلُوبُ ﴿٢٨﴾

Those who believe, and whose hearts find satisfaction in the remembrance of Allah: for without doubt in remembrance of Allah do hearts find satisfaction.

(al-Ra'd 13: 28)

Allah (*swt*) informs us in the Holy Qur'ān that all His Creation is engaged in His remembrance and praise. For example in *Sūrah al-Ḥashr* it is stated:

سَبَّحَ لِلَّهِ مَا فِى ٱلسَّمَـٰوَٰتِ وَمَا فِى ٱلْأَرْضِ ۖ وَهُوَ ٱلْعَزِيزُ ٱلْحَكِيمُ ﴿١﴾

Whatever is in the heavens and on earth glorifies Allah: For He is the Exalted in Might, the Wise.

(al-Ḥashr 59: 1)

It is only human beings who were given the freedom of choice to submit to the will of Allah or to follow their own desires. The difference between a Muslim and a non-Muslim is not in their physical appearance. Physically, they are the same. The real difference is that Muslims remember Allah, their Creator, and bow down to Him in submission. By these acts, Muslims achieve complete harmony with the entire universe and are at peace with themselves. This gives satisfaction of heart.

This *Dhikr* has to be at three levels. First, the seat of *Dhikr* is *Qalb* (heart). We should be conscious of the presence of Allah as much as possible and as the Qur'ān reminds us:

وَلَا تَكُن مِّنَ ٱلْغَـٰفِلِينَ ﴿٢٠٥﴾

And be not among those who are forgetful.
(al-Aʿrāf 7: 205)

Second, we should recite His praise and His glory with our tongues. This *Dhikr* should be with humility and reverence, without loudness of voice whether sitting, standing or lying down on our sides in the mornings or evenings, day or night. All other *'Ibādah* are quantified, for example in the times of Prayers, the days of fasting or the amount to be paid in *Zakāh*. But for *Dhikr*, Allah (*swt*) has set no limits. In several places in the Qur'ān we are exhorted to do *Dhikr* as much as possible:

يَـٰٓأَيُّهَا ٱلَّذِينَ ءَامَنُوا۟ ٱذْكُرُوا۟ ٱللَّهَ ذِكْرًا كَثِيرًا ﴿٤١﴾

O you who believe! Celebrate the praises of Allah, and do so often.
(al-Ahzāb 33: 41)

وَٱذْكُرُوا۟ ٱللَّهَ كَثِيرًا لَّعَلَّكُمْ تُفْلِحُونَ ﴿١٠﴾

And celebrate the praises of Allah often (and without stint) that you may prosper.
(al-Jumuʿah 62: 10)

It is the attributes of hypocrites that they do not remember Allah and pray without sincerity of heart:

إِنَّ ٱلْمُنَـٰفِقِينَ يُخَـٰدِعُونَ ٱللَّهَ وَهُوَ خَـٰدِعُهُمْ وَإِذَا قَامُوٓا۟ إِلَى ٱلصَّلَوٰةِ
قَامُوا۟ كُسَالَىٰ يُرَآءُونَ ٱلنَّاسَ وَلَا يَذْكُرُونَ ٱللَّهَ إِلَّا قَلِيلًا ﴿١٤٢﴾

The hypocrites – they think they are over-reaching Allah but He will over-reach them: when they stand up to Prayer, they stand without earnestness, to be seen by people, but little do they hold Allah in remembrance.

(al-Nisā' 4: 142)

Then, *Dhikr* should be with the presence of heart and mind and not merely a recitation of *Tasbīḥ* as a routine. Of course *Dhikr* can be in any language, but it is recommended to use the *Adhkār* which the Prophet (peace be upon him) and his Companions have prescribed. Thus, if *Dhikr* is in Arabic you should know what you are saying and the implications of so saying that. For example, if you recite *Subḥān Allāh* you should think that you are praising Allah and assert that He is above all imperfection. Similarly, saying *Al-Ḥamdu lil-Lāh* signifies that He is the only one Who is entitled to praise. All praises are for Him alone. And by reciting *Allāhu Akbar* you proclaim the greatness of our Creator. He is the most Majestic, High and Glorious. Thus *Dhikr* should be with *Fikr* (reflection).

Finally, *Dhikr* is not only with heart and tongue but our actions should also manifest what we think and say. When engaging in Jihād the instruction is:

يَٰٓأَيُّهَا ٱلَّذِينَ ءَامَنُوٓاْ إِذَا لَقِيتُمۡ فِئَةٗ فَٱثۡبُتُواْ وَٱذۡكُرُواْ ٱللَّهَ
كَثِيرٗا لَّعَلَّكُمۡ تُفۡلِحُونَ ٤٥

O you who believe! When you meet a force, be firm, and call Allah in remembrance much (and often); that you may prosper.

(al-Anfāl 8: 45)

Clearly to be firm and remembering Allah during Jihād is to persevere and to fight with valour and not to retreat.

In *Sūrah al-Munāfiqūn* Allah (*swt*) says:

يَٰٓأَيُّهَا ٱلَّذِينَ ءَامَنُواْ لَا تُلۡهِكُمۡ أَمۡوَٰلُكُمۡ وَلَآ أَوۡلَٰدُكُمۡ عَن ذِكۡرِ
ٱللَّهِۚ وَمَن يَفۡعَلۡ ذَٰلِكَ فَأُوْلَٰٓئِكَ هُمُ ٱلۡخَٰسِرُونَ ٩

O you who believe! Let not your riches or your children divert you from the remembrance of Allah. If any act thus, the loss is their own.

(al-Munāfiqūn 63: 9)

The following *āyah* states:

وَأَنفِقُواْ مِن مَّا رَزَقْنَـٰكُم مِّن قَبْلِ أَن يَأْتِىَ أَحَدَكُمُ ٱلْمَوْتُ

And spend something (in charity) out of the substance which We have bestowed on you, before death should come to any of you.

(al-Munāfiqūn 63: 10)

It is very evident that *Dhikr* here means *Infāq fī Sabīl Allāh*. Remembrance of Allah demands that a person should remember his death and spend his wealth in the way of Allah.

Thus, through *Dhikr* we establish our relationship with Allah (*swt*). This is the source of our strength. In a *ḥadīth qudsī* related by Abū Hurairah, the Prophet (peace be upon him) said: Allah Almighty says:

أَنَا عِنْدَ ظَنِّ عَبْدِي بِي وَأَنَا مَعَهُ إِذَا ذَكَرَنِي فَإِنْ ذَكَرَنِي فِي نَفْسِهِ ذَكَرْتُهُ فِي نَفْسِي وَإِنْ ذَكَرَنِي فِي مَلإٍ ذَكَرْتُهُ فِي مَلإٍ خَيْرٍ مِنْهُمْ وَإِنْ تَقَرَّبَ إِلَيَّ بِشِبْرٍ تَقَرَّبْتُ إِلَيْهِ ذِرَاعًا وَإِنْ تَقَرَّبَ إِلَيَّ ذِرَاعًا تَقَرَّبْتُ إِلَيْهِ بَاعًا وَإِنْ أَتَانِي يَمْشِي أَتَيْتُهُ هَرْوَلَةً

(متفق عليه)

I am as My servant expects Me to be. I am with him when he makes mention of Me. If he makes mention of Me to himself, I make mention of him to Myself; and if he makes mention of Me in an assembly, I make mention of him in an assembly better than it. And if he draws near to Me a hand's span, I draw near to him an

arm's length; and if he draws near to Me an arm's length,
I draw near to him a fathom's length. And if he comes to
Me walking, I go to him at speed.
(Bukhārī and Muslim)

How fortunate we are that if we remember Allah He remembers us and if we remember Him in a gathering He remembers us in a better gathering of angels. This should motivate us to engage in *Dhikr* as much as possible.

Dhikr acts as a regulator and a control mechanism in our lives. Remembrance of Allah keeps us on the Straight Path. If we deviate from it, remembrance of Allah brings us back to the Right Path. As the Holy Qur'ān says about *Ṣalāh*, which essentially is a higher form of *Dhikr*.

إِنَّ ٱلصَّلَوٰةَ تَنْهَىٰ عَنِ ٱلْفَحْشَآءِ وَٱلْمُنكَرِ

Indeed Prayer restrains one from shameful and unjust deeds.
(al-'Ankabūt 29: 45)

As I mentioned before, it creates harmony with other creations and particularly with angels who are always engaged in the *Dhikr* of Allah. Thus, *Dhikr* elevates human beings to the plane of *Malā'ikah* (angels).

There are many *Adhkār* which you can pick up from books of *aḥādīth*. I will mention a few of them which are very short and easy to remember and I hope you will at least recite them five times each after *Fajr* and *Maghrib* Prayers.

Let us pray that Allah may make us among those who remember Him constantly. (*Āmīn.*)

Adhkār for after *Fajr* and *Maghrib* Prayers

لاَ إِلَهَ إِلاَّ اللَّهُ وَحْدَهُ لاَ شَرِيكَ لَهُ لَهُ الْمُلْكُ وَلَهُ الْحَمْدُ
وَهُوَ عَلَى كُلِّ شَيْءٍ قَدِيرٌ

There is no god but Allah, One without partners,
dominion and praise are to Him and Allah has power
over all things.

سُبْحَانَ اللَّهِ وَالْحَمْدُ لِلَّهِ وَلاَ إِلَهَ إِلاَّ اللَّهُ وَاللَّهُ أَكْبَرُ وَلاَ حَوْلَ وَلاَ قُوَّةَ إِلاَّ بِاللَّهِ الْعَلِيِّ الْعَظِيمِ

Glory be to Allah; thankful Praises be to Allah; there is no god but Allah. Allah is the Greatest and there is neither effort nor strength except from Allah, the High and Mighty.

سُبْحَانَ اللَّهِ وَبِحَمْدِهِ سُبْحَانَ اللَّهِ الْعَظِيمِ

Glory with all Thankful Praise be to Allah, Glory be to Allah, the Mighty.

اللَّهُمَّ صَلِّ وَسَلِّمْ عَلَى عَبْدِكَ وَرَسُولِكَ وَحَبِيبِكَ سَيِّدِنَا مُحَمَّدٍ النَّبِيِّ الأُمِّيِّ وَعَلَى آلِهِ وَأَصْحَابِهِ وَبَارِكْ وَسَلِّمْ

O Allah! Salute, bless and pray on Your slave, Messenger and Beloved our lord Muḥammad, the unlettered Apostle, as well as his household and Companions. Bless him and grant peace to him.

رَبِّ اغْفِرْ وَارْحَمْ وَأَنْتَ خَيرُ الرَّاحِمِين

O Lord! Forgive me and have mercy on me, You are the best Mercy-Giver.

اللَّهُمَّ أَجِرْنِي مِنْ النَّارِ

O Allah! Protect me from the Hell-fire.

(*Āmīn.*)

Tawbah and *Istighfār*

وَتُوبُوٓاْ إِلَى ٱللَّهِ جَمِيعًا أَيُّهَ ٱلْمُؤْمِنُونَ لَعَلَّكُمْ تُفْلِحُونَ ﴿٣١﴾

And O you Believers! Repent you all together to Allah that you may attain Bliss.

(al-Nūr 24: 31)

وَٱسْتَغْفِرُواْ رَبَّكُمْ ثُمَّ تُوبُوٓاْ إِلَيْهِ ۚ إِنَّ رَبِّى رَحِيمٌ وَدُودٌ ﴿٩٠﴾

And seek forgiveness of your Lord, and turn unto Him in repentance, for my Lord is indeed full of mercy and loving-kindness.

(Hūd 11: 90)

We all desire to lead a successful and good life. We all know what we have to do to attain success. By success of course we mean success in this world and in the Hereafter. As Muslims this should be and must be our goal in life. That is why Allah (*swt*) has taught us to pray: "Our Lord! Grant us success in this world and in the Hereafter."

Why do we fail in our efforts? Who stops us from attaining our goals? If we ponder we will realise that we are our own worst enemy. We know what is good and what is evil. Yet we commit mistakes, we commit sins. We are determined to stay on the Right Path yet we slip. Having said this we should not be despondent. We cannot separate sin from man. It is like walking on water. We are bound to get wet. Allah is Merciful and He has provided a way for our salvation. That is repentance.

When we commit a mistake or a sin usually we have a feeling of guilt, of shame, and we regret that we have done it. If this remorse and guilt is present then there is hope that we can reform ourselves. When someone persistently keeps sinning without regret and remorse then all avenues of reform are closed.

قَالَ رَسُولُ اللَّهِ صَلَّى اللَّهُ عَلَيْهِ وَسَلَّمَ النَّدَمُ تَوْبَةٌ

(ابن ماجة)

The Prophet (peace be upon him) has said: "Remorse is a kind of repentance."

(Ibn Mājah)

Repentance after committing sin and promising one self not to do it again means that a person has reverted to piety. Thus, when he returns to piety Allah also returns to him with His mercy. *Tawbah* literally means to return. Thus, when we feel remorseful and guilty after committing a sin we should repent and have the determination to avoid sinning again. There should be sincerity in our repentance. This is termed as *Tawbatan Naṣūḥā*. Allah (*swt*) says:

يَـٰٓأَيُّهَا ٱلَّذِينَ ءَامَنُوا۟ تُوبُوٓا۟ إِلَى ٱللَّهِ تَوْبَةً نَّصُوحًا ... ﴿٨﴾

O you who believe! Turn to Allah with sincere repentance.

(al-Taḥrīm 66: 8)

Naṣīḥah in Arabic means sincerity and good faith. Thus, it means that there should not be any hypocrisy in it nor any showing off. A person should reform and purify himself in such a way that others may take example from him. Together with repentance we should also do *Istighfār* – this means seeking Allah's forgiveness and His mercy. As it is said in *Sūrah al-Nisā'*:

فَإِن تَابَا وَأَصْلَحَا فَأَعْرِضُوا۟ عَنْهُمَآ ۗ إِنَّ ٱللَّهَ كَانَ

تَوَّابًا رَّحِيمًا ﴿١٦﴾

If they repent and amend, leave them alone; for Allah is Oft-Returning, Most Merciful.

(al-Nisā' 4: 16)

وَٱسْتَغْفِرِ ٱللَّهَ ۖ إِنَّ ٱللَّهَ كَانَ غَفُورًا رَّحِيمًا ﴿١٠٦﴾

And seek forgiveness of Allah, for Allah is Oft-Forgiving and Most Merciful.

(al-Nisā' 4: 106)

It is narrated that 'Alī ibn Abī Ṭālib (may Allah be pleased with him) saw a Bedouin repenting very hastily. He remarked that this is *Tawbatul Kādhibīn* meaning a repentance of liars. That person then asked him what is proper repentance? 'Alī replied there are six essential requirements of repentance. First, there should be remorse for what wrong you have done. Second, you should fulfil the obligation that you have neglected. Third, you should restore the rights of those you have usurped. Fourth, you should seek forgiveness from those you hurt. Fifth, you should determine not to repeat your sin and finally, you should make your soul subservient to Allah's obedience. The pleasure you felt from sinning should be counterbalanced by real self-denial, so that your soul should suffer the pain of anguish (*Kashshāf*).

After repentance, we should seek Allah's pardon. Allah loves His servants who seek His forgiveness:

إِنَّ ٱللَّهَ يُحِبُّ ٱلتَّوَّٰبِينَ وَيُحِبُّ ٱلْمُتَطَهِّرِينَ ﴿٢٢٢﴾

Allah loves those who repent constantly and He loves those who keep themselves pure and clean.

(al-Baqarah 2: 222)

Allah's Mercy and His Love for the repentance of His servants is illustrated by the Prophet (peace be upon him) in his narrating a story of a person who lost his camel with all his provisions in a desert whilst asleep. When he woke up, he found his camel missing.

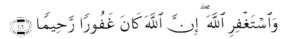

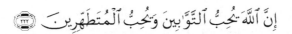

He searched everywhere but could not find it. Dejected, he lay down and went back to sleep thinking that he was surely going to die in this wilderness. Then he woke up again and he saw his camel fully laden with his provisions. His happiness knew no bounds and he was extremely grateful to Allah. The Prophet said that Allah would be far happier than this person would be if one of His servants were to repent (Muslim).

So what are the reasons for us not repenting and seeking Allah's forgiveness? Imām Ghazālī identified them as follows. First, we do not receive instant punishment for our sins. Thus, we feel relaxed, as we do not suffer any harm. Second, we get illicit pleasure in our sins. Third, we are too lazy to repent. Fourth, we hope Allah is Merciful and that He does not care about our sins. The final reason is our lack of firm belief in *Ākhirah* and our accountability before our Lord. He has suggested various remedies for overcoming these weaknesses. He states that we should realise that life is transitory and that we may die at any time, hence, we should not delay in repenting. Though we are often tempted to commit sins we should refrain from doing so. As we avoid eating food that we love if our doctors advise us that it is harmful, so our Creator deserves much more respect than our physician does. Finally, although God is Merciful, He has given us only one life. Our success will be determined by what we do in our lives.

We should always take account of our shortcomings and repent and seek Allah's mercy. It is reported by Abū Hurairah (may Allah be pleased with him) that he said I heard the Prophet (peace be upon him) saying: "By God I do *Istighfār* more than seventy times during a day" (Bukhārī). In another *ḥadīth* he is reported to have said: "O People repent to Allah and do *Istighfār* as I seek repentance a hundred times during a day" (Muslim). These *aḥādīth* highlight the importance of *Tawbah* and *Istighfār* and the practice of our beloved Prophet all of whose shortcomings were forgiven by Allah. Yet he was so conscious of his conduct that he constantly sought Allah's forgiveness and mercy. And we who commit sins all the time remain neglectful of our duty to repent and seek Allah's forgiveness!

We should follow the advice of Imām Nawawī. He says, first we should try and avoid sins and if we do commit them then we should feel ashamed. After repentance, we should promise never to commit the same sin again. And if the rights of others are violated then we should seek their forgiveness. Of course, we should always seek Allah's forgiveness and His mercy.

Let us pray that Allah (*swt*) gives us the *Tawfīq* to repent and seek His forgiveness and mercy throughout our life. (*Āmīn.*)

Brotherhood

إِنَّمَا ٱلْمُؤْمِنُونَ إِخْوَةٌ ... ﴿١٠﴾

The Believers are but a single Brotherhood.
(al-Ḥujurāt 49: 10)

On the authority of Abū Hurairah, (may Allah be pleased with him), who said: The Messenger of Allah (peace be upon him) said:

الْمُسْلِمُ أَخُو الْمُسْلِمِ لاَ يَظْلِمُهُ وَلاَ يَخْذُلُهُ وَلاَ يَحْقِرُهُ التَّقْوَى هَاهُنَا
وَيُشِيرُ إِلَى صَدْرِهِ ثَلاَثَ مَرَّاتٍ بِحَسْبِ امْرِئٍ مِنَ الشَّرِّ أَنْ يَحْقِرَ
أَخَاهُ الْمُسْلِمَ كُلُّ الْمُسْلِمِ عَلَى الْمُسْلِمِ حَرَامٌ دَمُهُ وَمَالُهُ وَعِرْضُهُ

(مسلم)

A Muslim is the brother of a Muslim: he neither oppresses him nor does he fail him, he neither lies to him nor does he hold him in contempt. Piety is right here – and he pointed to his breast three times. It is evil enough for a man to hold his Muslim brother in contempt. The whole of a Muslim for another Muslim is inviolable: his blood, his property, and his honour.

(Muslim)

It is the Mercy and blessing of Allah (*swt*) that He has brought us together in this Institution of Higher Education. The Muslim students here are but a microcosm of the Muslim *Ummah* at large. They represent different nationalities, languages, colours; schools of *Fiqh* as well as attachments to different organisations that are working for the revival of Islam. This is Allah's Mercy for which we should be grateful.

It is sad to see the internal strife currently plaguing the Muslim *Ummah*. We are witnessing civil war and bloodshed in many parts of the Muslim world – Muslims are unfortunately killing Muslims. In the same countries Muslim governments are oppressing and torturing Muslim masses. These rivalries which are dividing the Muslim *Ummah* are the product of different races, languages nationalities or Schools of *Fiqh*. We need unity among Muslims. By unity I do not mean uniformity. There will always be those who have a different approach. We should not try to steamroll everyone into following exactly the same pattern of behaviour as our own. As long as this pattern is permissible by the *Sharī'ah*, it is possible to have unity despite diversity.

The Prophet (peace be upon him) organised the Muslim society on the basis of brotherhood. Brotherhood means love, respect, sincerity, sympathy and mercy for those who share our beliefs. Brotherhood is an essential part of *Īmān*. The Prophet (peace be upon him) is reported to have said:

لاَ تُؤْمِنُوا حَتَّى تَحَابُّوا

(مسلم)

You are not *Mu'min* unless you love each other.
(Muslim)

Mu'ādh ibn Jabal said that the Prophet (peace be upon him) said:

قَالَ اللَّهُ عَزَّ وَجَلَّ وَجَبَتْ مَحَبَّتِي لِلْمُتَحَابِّينَ فِيَّ وَالْمُتَجَالِسِينَ فِيَّ
وَالْمُتَزَاوِرِينَ فِيَّ وَالْمُتَبَاذِلِينَ فِيَّ. إِنَّ اللَّهَ يَقُولُ يَوْمَ الْقِيَامَةِ أَيْنَ
الْمُتَحَابُّونَ بِجَلاَلِي الْيَوْمَ أُظِلُّهُمْ فِي ظِلِّي يَوْمَ لاَ ظِلَّ إِلاَّ ظِلِّي

(احمد)

Allah says My love is imperative for those who love each other for My sake, who sit together for My sake, who travel to meet each other for My sake and those who spend on each other for My sake. Allah will say on

the Day of Resurrection where are those who love one
another through My glory. Today, I shall give them
shelter in My shelter, whereas there is no shelter
except My shelter.

(Bukhārī)

Love of our brothers for the sake of Allah (*swt*) is the bond that we have to seek. It is a bounty of Allah and it is given only to those who endeavour to seek it. Allah (*swt*) says to the Prophet (peace be upon him) that it is only His mercy that joined the hearts of Muslims:

وَأَلَّفَ بَيْنَ قُلُوبِهِمْ ۚ لَوْ أَنفَقْتَ مَا فِي ٱلْأَرْضِ جَمِيعًا مَّآ أَلَّفْتَ بَيْنَ
قُلُوبِهِمْ وَلَٰكِنَّ ٱللَّهَ أَلَّفَ بَيْنَهُمْ ۚ إِنَّهُۥ عَزِيزٌ حَكِيمٌ ﴿٦٣﴾

*God is the One Who united their hearts, had you
expended all the riches of the earth, you could not have
united their hearts together, but God united them,
indeed He is Almighty, All Wise.*

(al-Anfāl 8: 63)

So how do you cultivate *Ukhuwwah* – brotherly relationship? The most important quality required is sincerity. You should prefer the same for your brother that you prefer for yourself. The examples from the *Sīrah* of the Prophet (peace be upon him) and his Companions (may Allah be pleased with them) show how sincere they were towards their fellow Muslims. The story of the *Muhājirūn* and the *Anṣār* and their mutual love and concern seems exemplary.

The other attribute is a willingness to sacrifice for the sake of others. We read the story of a Companion of the Prophet that when a guest came to his house and there was not enough food in the house he and his family went hungry so that the guest could be fed. We read the story of those wounded in the Battle of Yarmūk who were crying out for water. When water was brought to one of them and he heard the request from his brother he refused to drink and asked that water be taken to his brother first who again passed it on to the next. In the end, all died without drinking water.

Mercy is also needed to develop our affection for others. It has, though, to be a complete and overflowing mercy. Allah, addressing the Prophet in the Holy Qur'ān, says:

فَبِمَا رَحْمَةٍ مِّنَ ٱللَّهِ لِنتَ لَهُمْ ۖ وَلَوْ كُنتَ فَظًّا غَلِيظَ ٱلْقَلْبِ لَٱنفَضُّوا۟
مِنْ حَوْلِكَ ۖ فَٱعْفُ عَنْهُمْ وَٱسْتَغْفِرْ لَهُمْ ... ﴿١٥٩﴾

It was God's Mercy that you were kind to them, had you been harsh and hard of heart, they would have dispersed from around you, so pardon them, and pray for forgiveness for them...

(Āl ʿImrān 3: 159)

It is narrated by Jābir ibn ʿAbdullāh (may Allah be pleased with him) that the Prophet (peace be upon him) arrived just as the body of ʿAbdullāh ibn Ubayy was being placed in the grave. The Prophet asked that his body be taken out of it. Then he placed his body upon his own knees and put his saliva in ʿAbdullāh ibn Ubayy's mouth and put his own shirt on his body (Bukhārī and Muslim).

Here, we see the Prophet's mercy for ʿAbdullāh ibn Ubayy, leader of the hypocrites. So his love and mercy for true believers must be boundless!

Finally, a readiness to forgive the shortcomings and faults of others should be an essential trait of our character. We see from the *Sīrah* of the Prophet how kind and forgiving he was. One of the Companions wanted to send a letter informing the Quraysh about the planned conquest of Makkah by the Prophet. The reason being his family was in Makkah and he wanted to ensure their safety. When the letter was intercepted, the Companions wanted him punished but the Prophet forgave his shortcomings. Then in the Battle of Uḥud he asked a group of Companions to remain at their post but when they saw that the Muslims were gaining victory, they left their post with the result that the Quraysh took the advantage and attacked the Muslim army from the rear and victory turned into defeat. But the Prophet forgave the Companions who disobeyed his instructions. He also forgave Hind, the wife of Abū Sufyān when she accepted Islam. She was the one who ate the liver of the Prophet's beloved uncle, 'Abbās, who was martyred in the Battle of Uḥud.

It is worth recalling the words of wisdom of Ustādh Ḥasan al-Bannā' Shahīd (may Allah have mercy on him). He writes:

> By brotherhood, I mean that your heart and soul are firmly tied with true Faith, because Faith creates the most precious relationship. Brotherhood is the brotherhood in Faith. The primary strength is unity and unity cannot be achieved without love. The smallest part of love is that your heart should be without malice towards your brother and the highest rank is to sacrifice yourself for his sake.

Let us pray that Allah may create true love and brotherhood among us. All our disagreement and differences are resolved by brotherly love and understanding. (*Āmīn.*)

The Muslim *Ummah*

قُلِ ٱللَّهُمَّ مَٰلِكَ ٱلْمُلْكِ تُؤْتِى ٱلْمُلْكَ مَن تَشَآءُ وَتَنزِعُ ٱلْمُلْكَ مِمَّن تَشَآءُ وَتُعِزُّ مَن تَشَآءُ وَتُذِلُّ مَن تَشَآءُ ۖ بِيَدِكَ ٱلْخَيْرُ ۖ إِنَّكَ عَلَىٰ كُلِّ شَىْءٍ قَدِيرٌ ﴿٢٦﴾

Say: "O Allah! Lord of Power (and Rule), You give power to whom You please. And You strip off power from whom You please. You exalt whom You please and You abase whom You please. In Your Hand is all Good. Verily, over all things You have power.

(Āl 'Imrān 3: 26)

Every fifth person in the world is a Muslim. There are 56 independent Muslim countries with enormous natural and human resources at their disposal. There are more than one billion Muslims in the world today and, if they are united, they can be a mighty force to shape the destiny of this *Ummah*. Alas, the reality is that the Muslim *Ummah* today is in a state of disarray. Muslim states are all at loggerheads just as they are divided into different nationalities, tribal loyalties and linguistic groupings. They are unable to act effectively as one *Ummah* – a concerted Muslim Nation.

Just reflect on the few events of the last decade:

- The war in Bosnia killing hundreds of thousands of innocent Muslims, men, women and children.
- The destruction of the three-centuries-old Babri Mosque in Ajodyha, India, by militant Hindu extremists.

- Bloodshed on a large scale in Chechnya.
- The bombing of Iraq by Western powers killing thousands of innocent people.
- The atrocities of the Indian Army in Kashmir where thousands of people have been tortured and killed.
- The continuing violence in Palestine where, every day, Muslims are being harassed and killed by the Israeli army.
- Serb oppression in Kosovo has claimed thousands of Muslim lives and the destruction of entire villages.

In spite of facing so many external threats and hostilities, the Muslims themselves are engaged in killing each other in many parts of the world – in Afghanistan, Algeria, Indonesia, Pakistan, Turkey and many other places. Instead of uniting to face the enemy and repelling the aggressors, we are hell bent on killing each other. Even mosques and the sacred month of Ramaḍān cannot stop us from these suicidal acts of folly.

It is always instructive to look back to our own history and try to learn lessons from it. So let us see the situation of the Muslim *Ummah* in the fifth century Hijrah, that is the eleventh century of the Common Era. It was on Friday 23rd Sha'bān 492 Hijrah, corresponding to the year 1099, that Christian Crusaders stormed the Holy City of Jerusalem. Seventy thousand worshippers, men, women, children and the elderly, were slaughtered. The Crusaders looted the priceless historical treasures from the Baitul Maqdis.

Contemporary historians have written that Duke Godfrey of Bouillon and Tancred of Hauteville rode through the streets of Jerusalem choked with the dead and dying. Hundreds of Muslims were tortured, burned and slain in cold blood, a wanton massacre. Their reign of terror continued for 90 years.

Will and Ariel Durant in their book *The Story of Civilisation* record:

> Women were stabbed to death, suckling babes were snatched by the leg from mothers' breasts and flung over the walls or had their necks broken by being dashed against posts and seventy thousand Moslems remaining in the city were slaughtered.

Imām Ibn Kathīr (may the mercy of Allah be upon him) in his book on *Jihād* reflected on these tragic events and enumerates the following reasons for the defeat of the Muslims:

> Firstly the Islamic *Khilāfah* headed by the Fatimid Dynasty in Egypt, was weakened by internal dissension. Secondly, there was corruption prevalent in high places in Muslim society. And, finally, there were intrigues and conspiracies in the Court. Of course with these internal problems they could not succeed against their enemy.

This was the terrible state of affairs of this *Ummah* when Ṣalāḥuddīn Ayyūbī came to power in one of the small kingdoms. He studied the political climate around him and with wisdom and sagacity tried to solve the problem. He undertook the following remedial strategy: first he took effective measures to get rid of corrupt officials from his government. Then he replaced the old guard and replaced the Fatimid Dynasty. Finally, he unified the *Ummah* under his leadership.

Thus, in the next Crusade when there was another encounter between Christians and Muslim armies, the Crusaders were defeated and Ṣalāḥuddīn recaptured the Holy City of Jerusalem.

After reviewing this victorious conquest of Jerusalem, Ibn Kathīr wrote:

> Any further Crusades will be defeated as this *Ummah* has learnt the lesson from its defeat.

But have we learnt the lesson? How did we lose Palestine again? If we were to analyse our defeat we would find the same causes.

Like the Fatimid *Khilāfah*, the 'Uthmānī *Khilāfah* was weak. Turkey was referred to as the "Sick man of Europe". Then there was rampant corruption in Muslim society and of course there was disunity among the Muslims. The West was able to exploit this. Using spies like Lawrence of Arabia and Glubb Pasha it created hatred and enmity between Turks and Arabs.

So what lessons we have to learn from our own history! The Holy Qur'ān has extensively used historical events to illustrate and remind us that events do not just happen but that it is Allah (*swt*) who controls our destinies. There is no blind force that governs human affairs but there are Divine laws that settle the destinies of nations. What are these laws and how can we acquire that insight so that we can understand and interpret all the events happening all around us?

Let us briefly reflect on these laws as enunciated in the Holy Qur'ān:

Allah is Just and He likes justice to prevail in the world. Allah does not like corruption. This is mentioned in very many places in the Holy Qur'ān:

وَيَسْعَوْنَ فِي ٱلْأَرْضِ فَسَادًا ۚ وَٱللَّهُ لَا يُحِبُّ ٱلْمُفْسِدِينَ ﴿٦٤﴾

Their effort is for corruption in the land and Allah does not love those who are corrupt.

(al-Mā'idah 5: 64)

Hence, a corrupt regime, whether it is run by non-Muslims or so-called Muslims, is bound to be disgraced and replaced by those who are relatively better than the perpetrators of such corruption.

Allah (*swt*) has sent His Messengers to establish justice in this world. Their mission is stated as follows in the Holy Qur'ān:

لَقَدْ أَرْسَلْنَا رُسُلَنَا بِٱلْبَيِّنَٰتِ وَأَنزَلْنَا مَعَهُمُ ٱلْكِتَٰبَ
وَٱلْمِيزَانَ لِيَقُومَ ٱلنَّاسُ بِٱلْقِسْطِ ... ﴿٢٥﴾

Indeed We sent forth Messengers with clear Revelations and We sent down with them the Book and the Balance, so that mankind may establish justice.

(al-Ḥadīd 57: 25)

As this *Ummah* is now singularly failing to perform its duty, we are breaching our covenant with Allah. The present pathetic condition in which we find ourselves is a consequence of being deprived of Allah's Blessings. Events that are happening are reminders for us to realise our mistakes and return to our assigned duty.

So how can a unifying personality like Salāḥuddīn Ayyūbī emerge? The signs are not very encouraging. Yet we should never be pessimistic. If we really want to bring about a change in our situation we have to start the change from within ourselves. Allah helps those who help themselves. As Allah says in the Holy Qur'ān:

إِنَّ ٱللَّهَ لَا يُغَيِّرُ مَا بِقَوْمٍ حَتَّىٰ يُغَيِّرُوا۟ مَا بِأَنفُسِهِمْ ... ﴿١١﴾

Verily never will Allah change the condition of a people until they change it themselves (with their own souls).

(al-Ra'd 13: 11)

There is a saying that explains the different attitudes people adopt:

> There are those who make things happen. There are those who watch things happen and there are those who say, "What has happened?"

Let us hope and pray that we are those who can make history and do not become history. May Allah unite us and make us realise our prime duty to earnestly embark upon our mission in this world. (*Āmīn.*)

First *Khuṭbah*

الْحَمْدُ لِلَّهِ نَحْمَدُهُ وَنَسْتَعِينُهُ وَنَسْتَغْفِرُهُ وَنُؤْمِنُ بِهِ وَنَتَوَكَّلُ عَلَيْهِ – وَنَعُوذُ بِاللَّهِ مِنْ شُرُورِ أَنْفُسِنَا وَسَيِّئَاتِ أَعْمَالِنَا – مَنْ يَهْدِهِ اللَّهُ فَلا مُضِلَّ لَهُ وَمَنْ يُضْلِلْهُ فَلا هَادِيَ لَهُ – وَنَشْهَدُ أَنْ لا إِلَهَ إِلاَّ اللَّهُ وَحْدَهُ لا شَرِيكَ لَهُ – وَنَشْهَدُ أَنَّ مُحَمَّدًا عَبْدُهُ وَرَسُولُهُ – أَرْسَلَهُ بِالْحَقِّ بَشِيراً وَنَذِيراً بَيْنَ يَدَيْ السَّاعَةِ – مَنْ يُطِعْ اللهَ وَرَسُولَهُ فَقَدْ رَشَدَ وَاهْتَدَى وَمَنْ يَعْصِهِمَا فَإِنَّهُ قَدْ غَوَى – وَأَنَّهُ لا يَضُرُّ إلاَّ نَفْسَهُ وَلا يَضُرُّ اللهَ شَيْئاً – إِنَّ أَصْدَقَ الْحَدِيثِ كِتَابُ اللَّهِ وَأَحْسَنَ الْهَدْيِ هَدْيُ مُحَمَّدٍ صَلَّى اللهُ عَلَيْهِ وَسَلَّمْ – وَأَنَّ خَيْرَ الأُمُورِ عَوَازِمُهَا وَشَرَّ الأُمُورِ مُحْدَثَاتُهَا، وَكُلُّ مُحْدَثَةٍ بِدْعَةٌ وَكُلُّ بِدْعَةٍ ضَلالَةٌ وَكُلُّ ضَلالَةٍ فِي النَّارِ. أَمَّا بَعْدُ، فَأَعُوذُ بِاللهِ مِنَ الشَّيْطَانِ الرَّجِيمِ – بِسْمِ اللهِ الرَّحْمَنِ الرَّحِيمِ – قَالَ اللهُ تَعَالَى فِي كِتَابِهِ الْمَجِيدِ. . .*

Thankful praise be to Allah (*swt*). We thank and praise Allah seeking His help and His Forgiveness. We believe in Him and we have our trust in Him. We seek His refuge from the evil of our carnal self and from our sinful actions. Whomsoever Allah has guided no one can

* Please recite the *āyah* from the *Khuṭbah* you have chosen to deliver.

lead him astray and whomsoever Allah has misguided no one can guide him. We bear witness that there is no deity except Allah and He is One and there are no partners with Him. We bear witness that Muḥammad is His servant and Messenger (peace be upon him). He was sent as a bearer of glad Tidings and as a warner before the coming of the Hour. The one who obeys Allah and His Messenger he is guided and achieves righteousness and he who disobeys them has transgressed. He does not harm anyone but himself and he does not harm Allah at all. Certainly the best discourse is the Book of Allah and the best guidance is the guidance of Muḥammad. The peace and blessings of Allah be on him. The best deeds are firm and balanced acts and evil deeds are novel acts and new things introduced in the *Dīn*. All novel acts are innovations and all innovations are spurious and misguided and all misguided are in the Fire.

I seek refuge with Allah from the accursed Satan. I begin in the Name of Allah, the Merciful, the Beneficent. *Allāh Ta'ālā* says in his Glorious Book...**

** Please read the translation of the *āyah*.

Second *Khuṭbah*

اَلْحَمْدُ لِلّٰهِ رَبِّ الْعَالَمِينَ - وَالصَّلَاةُ وَالسَّلَامُ عَلَى رَسُولِهِ الْأَمِينِ -
اَمَا بَعْدُ فَيَا مَعْشَرَ الْمُسْلِمِينَ - أَعُوذُ بِاللهِ مِنَ الشَّيْطَانِ الرَّجِيمِ -
بِسْمِ اللهِ الرَّحْمَنِ الرَّحِيمِ - قَالَ اللهُ تَعَالَى فِي كِتَابِهِ الْكَرِيمِ - إِنَّ
اللَّهَ وَمَلَائِكَتَهُ يُصَلُّونَ عَلَى النَّبِيِّ يَا أَيُّهَا الَّذِينَ آمَنُوا صَلُّوا عَلَيْهِ
وَسَلِّمُوا تَسْلِيمًا — اللَّهُمَ صَلِّ عَلَى سَيِدِنَا وَمَوْلَانَا مُحَمَدٍ بِعَدَدِ مَنْ
صَلَّى وَصَامَ — اللَّهُمَ صَلِ عَلَى سَيِدِنَا وَمَوْلَانَا مُحَمَّدٍ بِعَدَدِ مَنْ
قَعَدَ وَقَامَ — اللَّهُمَ صَلِ عَلَى جَمِيعِ اللأَنْبِيَاءِ وَالْمُرْسَلِينَ وَعَلَى سَائِرِ
الصَحَابَةِ وَالتَّابِعِينَ وَعَلَى عِبَادَكَ الصَالِحِينَ — اللَّهُمَ أَيِّد الإِسْلَامَ
وَالْمُسْلِمِينَ — اللَّهُمَ انْصُرْ مَنْ نَصَرَ دِينَ مُحَمَّدٍ صَلَى اللهُ عَلَيْهِ وَسَلَمَ
وَاجْعَلْنَا مِنْهُمْ، وَاخْذُلْ مَنْ خَذَلَ دِينَ مُحَمَّدٍ صَلَّى اللهُ عَلَيْهِ وَسَلَّمَ
وَلاَ تَجْعَلْنَا مِنْهُمْ ، اللَّهُمَ أَرِنَا الحَقَ حَقاً وَارْزُقْنَا اتِّبَاعَهُ وَارِنَا البَاطِلَ
بَاطِلاً وَارْزُقْنَا اجْتِنَابَهُ — اللَّهُمَ ثَبِّتْنَا عَلَى الإِسْلَامِ — اللَّهُمَّ نَوِّرْ قُلُوبَنَا
بِنُورِ الإِيمَانَ — اللَّهُمَّ اَغْفِرِ لِلْمُؤْمِنِينَ وَالْمُؤْمِنَات — الأَحْيَاءِ مِنْهُمْ
وَالأَمْوَاتِ — عِبَادَ اللهِ رَحِمَكُمُ اللهُ إِنَّ اللَّهَ يَأْمُرُ بِالْعَدْلِ وَالإِحْسَانِ
وَإِيتَاءِ ذِي الْقُرْبَى وَيَنْهَى عَنْ الْفَحْشَاءِ وَالْمُنْكَرِ وَالْبَغْيِ يَعِظُكُمْ
لَعَلَّكُمْ تَذَكَّرُونَ — اُذْكُرُوا اللهَ يَذْكُرْكُمْ وَادْعُوهُ يَسْتَجِبْ لَكُمْ —
وَلَذِكْرُ اللهِ تَعَالَىٰ اَعْلَىٰ وَاَوْلَىٰ وَأَعَزُّ وَاَجَلُّ وَاَتَمُّ وَاَهَمُّ وَاَكْبَرُ —

Praise be to Allah the Cherisher and Sustainer of the worlds. Peace, blessings and salutations are on His trustworthy Messenger. O Assembly of Muslims! I seek refuge with Allah from the accursed Satan. I begin in the name of Allah, the Merciful, the Beneficent. *Allāh Ta'ālā* has said in His Exalted Book, "Allah and His Angels send blessings on the Prophet: O you who believe send your blessings on him and salute him with respect." O Allah! Bless our master and our leader Muḥammad equal in number to those who pray and fast. O Allah! Bless our master and our leader Muḥammad equal in numbers to those who sit and stand. O Allah! Bless all Prophets and Messengers and bless all Companions and their successors and bless all Your pious servants. O Allah! Help those who help Islam and Muslims and make us amongst them and destroy those who destroy Islam and Muslims and do not make us amongst them. O Allah! Show us the truth as truth and make us obey it and show us the falsehood as falsehood and save us from it. O Allah! Keep us steadfast on Islam. O Allah! Brighten our hearts with the light of *Īmān*. O Allah! Forgive all believing men and women, alive or dead.

O servants of Allah! May Allah have His mercy on you. Allah commands justice, the doing of good, and liberality to kith and kin, and He forbids all shameful deeds, injustice and rebellion: He instructs you that you may receive admonition. Remember Allah and He will remember you and pray to Him and He will respond. Remembrance of *Allāh Ta'ālā* is the Highest, the foremost, the most honourable, the everlasting, the most important and the greatest.